The Purity of Jazz and Speckled Trout and Other Prose and Poetry

D1560155

The Purity of Jazz and Speckled Trout and Other Prose and Poetry

JAMES ROBERT CAMPBELL

gatekeeper press

Published by Gatekeeper Press
3971 Hoover Rd. Suite 77
Columbus, OH 43123-2839

Layout Design by: Mr. Merwin D. Loquias

ISBN: 9781619845169

Printed in the United States of America

Contents

For
Kiera Thomas
I appreciate your interest in my work.
Tom
Campbell
4-15-17

Some of these sixteen stories have appeared in TPQ Online, Falling Star, Refraction, Ascent Aspirations, The Cortland Review and Big Bridge.

ESCAPE OF THE FOXES

The foxes had unwisely dug a lair in an irrigation ditch because the soil was moist and soft and a great place for the female to have her kits. It was a big one with two entrances twelve feet apart. There had been some rain in the early fall and the dark green cotton was well-established and tall. The farmer thereby did not irrigate and immediately bring their habitation to disaster.

Nocturnal and cautious, they avoided notice until one early evening when the male was near the house on the northern hill, scouting chickens, and the farmer saw him running away. The sardonic little man in khakis and a stained felt cowboy hat looked for the lair the next day, a Friday, and upon finding it decided to drown them out by starting the well engine a half-mile away and flooding the ditch.

One of his best friends, the blacksmith-welder in Victory, was bringing his wife and children the next night for supper and canasta and he had the man and his son come early to help get rid of the foxes. He got a wire cage for his grandson and the blacksmith›s boy to hold over the second entrance on the north side of the ditch as the water coursed into the first. He thought the foxes must have kits and hoped both adults would run into the cage.

The boys knew they could be bitten unless they held the cage dead center over the hole and the foxes had nowhere else to go. The unmuffled irrigation engine started and here came the water, scuttling down the ditch and then pouring into the hole.

They were startled when the female, little and red, burst out over the water and got away south into the cotton. But sure enough, the cage shivered and filled with the bigger male and the farmer›s grandson pulled the cage up just enough to close the door and wire it shut. Wild as anything they had ever seen, the fox was caught. The cage had a handle, but he did not seem inclined to bite the older blacksmith›s boy›s hand as they walked to the dirt road to avoid trampling any cotton and made their way toward the old adobe farmhouse. It was almost dark and after the boys and their sisters had looked at the fox for awhile, it was mostly forgotten while they ate and then played hide and seek among ancient elm trees in front of the house.

Invisible in the south field but not far away, the female yipped. The male had no interest in anything but getting away, but it was a good cage and the door was secure. The blacksmith›s boy was unsure of the fox›s value to the men or the other boy. He went to the front porch a couple of times and watched it staring into the field and sometimes yipping back hysterically. He understood the need to drive them away, but he was sorry the kits were dead and they were separated. He had never liked seeing dogs chained or fenced and felt acutely now that wild things should run free. He went inside to see if any of the grownups were interested in the fox, but they were convivially playing their card game. He starting thinking no one would care much if he let it go because the foxes would surely leave the farm now.

He had shot a lot of birds and rabbits and sometimes considered his choice to shoot or not. He had usually shot and rarely missed, but the sense of responsibility was much greater with this bigger, more sentient animal--miserable and doomed because the farmer had no reason to let it go. The farmer would probably do something with the pelt because it was young and its fur was good.

No one else was around the porch. The boy felt he would always be happy with letting the foxes reunite and go on their fugitive way, but it was more with a sense of imperative that he moved to the cage and reached down. Fixated on the darkness, the fox paid no attention as he unfastened the wire, quietly opened the door and stepped back. It bolted with the same astonishing speed its mate had displayed and the boy imagined its running to her and their briefly licking each other›s faces before scampering away in the night, where the richly scented Texas Panhandle air swathed the countryside under the moonless sky.

MONICA'S APPLES

Monica believed Jesus was in the orchard because she bit an apple and it made her stop feeling there was a snake striking at her ankles. She liked to get home early from school and watch Alfredo because of the way he walked, sauntering and happy. She gave him a note in the hall, asking, "Do you like me?"

He did not answer but the next day smiled. She went into the orchard that night and Alfredo stepped from behind a tree and said, "Yes, I like you."

She knew little of love and tentatively reached out and entwined his fingers with hers. It was cool and a light breeze made her legs cold under her dress. Alfredo did not try to kiss her and she did not know how to get him to; so they sat by a tree and he took off his jacket and put it around her shoulders.

"I watched you walking," she said.

He was excited because she was pretty and he had never talked to her. "From your house?"

"From in there, yeah. You seem happy."

"Are you?"

"I'm afraid."

"Of what?"

"The devil. I have bad dreams."

"Did you tell the priest?"

"No, but I prayed and Jesus told me to eat an apple. I did and I felt better."

"Is that why you came here, to get an apple?"

"Not tonight. I just wanted to. Why did you?"

Alfredo had been going to look into her window but of course did not want to say so. "I don't know."

"Did you come here before?"

"No."

"Have you ever been in trouble?"

"No."

He was on probation for stealing CD's from a music store and had been caught vandalizing a teacher's car. "Do you want to be my girlfriend?"

"I don't know. Do you want to be my boyfriend?"

"Will you give me a kiss?"

"You can kiss me," she said, closing her eyes and puckering her lips. His jacket was getting her warm and she felt better, sitting there a short way into the orchard of one hundred trees. There were some birds fluttering around and a yellow cat nearby, looking up at them.

Alfredo and Monica started meeting every third night. His single mother let him roam, but her parents were more vigilant with her and her brother and sister. She had been going there for twenty or thirty minutes at a time before meeting Alfredo and their trysts were shorter at first as they began, then longer. They would embrace and kiss, but she would not let him do more and they mostly talked between their meetings and partings.

Honor was important to both of them and besides, she was a virgin. Alfredo told her he was, but he wasn't. His street gang he had set him up with a girl who hung out with the gang and smoked pot with them. He had been thinking he might end up going to prison and to avoid that, he was going to join the Army.

"Aren't you scared you might get killed?"

"No, not really." He was a little, considering the prospect of oblivion, but it was more important to be brave. That was more important than anything.

"What if I love you, Alfredo?"

"I guess you could wait for me."

"Would you marry me first?»

"Sure, I'd marry you." Monica was good and he had been thinking he loved her. They were going to let their parents and everyone at school know she was his girlfriend. He was sixteen and she was fifteen. They could get married just before he went into the Army, he thought. He had seen boys from Victory come back bigger and stronger with their dark green dress uniforms on and manly pride in their eyes.

"Jesus told me that if we eat an apple together, He will come into your soul and you'll never be bad again," she said.

"Okay, let's eat one then," he said, getting up from beside a tree with a thick trunk.

It was summertime in the Texas Panhandle and the apples were sweet. She picked one, rubbed it with the hem of her dress and bit into it. "It's good," she said.

It was indeed the best apple he had ever tasted. They took turns eating it until only the core was left and then they kissed in the soft shadows of the moonlight. Love poured into Alfredo's heart and for the first time in his life, he felt pure joy.

THE FIRST JACK

The boy and his daddy had had other dogs. There was Duke the half-coyote who could climb a ladder at the lumber yard but was poisoned by a hateful neighbor. There was little yellow Susie, who had litter after litter and whose teats hung halfway to the ground when she was nursing. Susie was a source of astonishment to some beautiful high school girls who found the boy›s explanation, "She has puppies," inadequate. There was the second Duke, whose left front leg was snapped when he ran in front of the big black Buick of some family friends in the driveway late one winter afternoon. They had his leg set and a cast put on, but he chewed it off and ended up having to be euthanized. A lot of things can happen to a dog, the boy had learned.

There was the second Jack a couple of years later, a trained Weimaraner who limped into Victory footsore and evidently lost from a hunting party. The city maintenance men knew the boy and his daddy were bird hunters and gave them the Weimaraner. He was a great dog, retrieving doves and ducks, swimming out with his webbed feet and pointing and retrieving quail. The boy started a game in which Jack carried dead birds by their heads as he ran up happily. The boy pulled the birds away and left the heads in Jack's mouth for him to chew them up, grinning his big doggy grin.

Daddy liked to hunt because he was an ex-Marine who had fought on Bougainville, Guam and other islands. He was excellent with any type of gun. They had lived in the country when the boy was in the second grade, and that was when he saw his daddy could do extraordinary things with guns. They lived about a hundred yards from the dirt road, and there was an old mangy cur dog who lived wild and had been coming around looking for things to eat. The boy was playing by the road and saw the dog coming, moving pretty fast with his tongue hanging out. He knew it would come to him and he did not want it to because it was dirty. Then he saw Daddy stepping quickly out of the house with his rifle, an eight-millimeter Mauser bolt-action, hurriedly wrap the sling around his left arm and take aim. The dog was fifteen or twenty yards in front of the boy when the rifle went "blooey!" and the dog collapsed on his jaw and the top of his skull went spinning up like a furry flying saucer--some distance up, though not as high as the top of the adjacent telephone pole, as it had seemed then.

The first Jack was a Boxer given to Daddy by a friend. Daddy was a blacksmith-welder who owned a large shop in town that his daddy, known to the family as Papa, had established in the early 1930's. The second Jack was Daddy›s dog, but the first Jack was the boy›s. He was big for a Boxer with terrific vitality and alertness. They started keeping dog food at the shop, different kinds of meat because Jack was still growing and always hungry. When they weren't working on trailers or tractors or heating plow points red in the forge and sharpening them with the triphammer and beveling them on the big-belted grinder, the boy would open a can or two and knock the meat out with the heel of his hand and let Jack catch it, chomp it three or four times and swallow it.

The boy got the bat game going like the bird heads game with the second Jack. They had a baseball, some gloves and a bat because Daddy had once been a pitcher--a talent that helped him survive the war as a valued hand grenade-throwing specialist. Thirteen or fourteen, the boy would get the bat from behind the triphammer and start Jack to biting it. He had the idea of strengthening the dog's neck, but he never jerked it around too hard because Daddy said to be careful and not break his teeth. However, as Jack grew bigger and stronger and the boy more adept, the game got more violent. Jack loved the bat game. He never brought the bat, wanting to play as some dogs would, but came running every time the boy brandished it.

The game took on an ineffable character as the boy learned his part and Jack became so powerful. He attacked as though killing a deer, barking and growling ferociously. He launched into it with complete ferocity, slobber flying as he assaulted it with his hind legs working like a fast-stepping prizefighter and his head snapping from side to side on his bulging neck. He crunched it so hard that the splinters would be falling onto the dirt floor between the forge room and the trailer room with the big sliding door that opened to the paved road outside. Jack bit and shook so hard that the boy's arms would be jerking around and he could barely hold on. They kept it up until the bat barrel was all chewed up and getting thinner and men started gathering around to watch. They began getting requests. Four or five men would be in the shop, one would say something to Daddy and he would say, "Go get the bat."

The boy knew dogs because he fed them, creosote-dipped them in a big hole in the backyard, bobbed and sutured their tails when they were puppies, poured raw eggs down their throats when they were sick and wept when they died. He understood that behind their domesticity and love of people, they had wild hearts and could lose their composure. That was why Jack would bite higher and higher on the handle and the boy would let go to avoid having his fingers bitten. As soon as the bat became inanimate, Jack lost interest and trotted away. They prized him a lot. So it was with long-lasting consternation that he disappeared and they realized he had been stolen. The boy remembered the semi-circles of men who had watched and knew it must have been one of them. He had never paid attention; they were just anonymous shadows in his memory.

Without ever saying who had done it, Daddy said somebody saw a pickup stop beside the shop, pick Jack up and drive off with him. A little while later, he told the boy he had learned who it was and gone there. It was some sort of gangster farmer who lived south of the nearby Destry. They had been stripping cotton when Daddy drove up and got out, saw Jack and said, "I believe that's my dog."

"No, he ain't," the farmer said. "We had him since he was a pup."

Daddy did not back off easily, but the man had a hired hand jump down from a cotton trailer and drive him away with a pitchfork. The boy thought Daddy would have gone to the sheriff if the farmer had stolen something of more tangible value; but as much as he liked Jack, it was not important enough to make it a public issue.

There no more dialogue about it for a few years, but the boy sometimes pictured Jack in the farmer's possession and felt hot resentment. They now had the second Jack, who was actually much more useful, and kept him in a pen or the fenced backyard to obviate a repetition. But the first Jack was never far from the boy's consciousness. One day when they were feeling cordial, he asked with false offhandedness, "So who stole Jack?"

Daddy looked at him with alarm and said, "No! I don't want you going out there."

BONES AND BRACELETS

The hall was narrow between the patients' knees. The lighting was poor and the air warm with the breath of the sick. The patients were mostly elderly and children accompanied by young and middle-age adults who docilely awaited the doctor. Their voices mixed and were lost in one another.

A woman sat among children who in turn looked warily at her and made faces ridiculing her. She was keeping her eyes half-closed, but occasionally she heard them, looked and smiled. She wasn't sure she should have come. She was not sick but had felt uneasy since early morning, when she woke up sweating and frightened. A lot of old women come in just for company, she thought, so the doctor might think her foolish.

A nurse called her name from a clipboard and for a moment she did not recognize the familiar syllables, then with an embarrassed start she tensed to rise. Pain gripped her chest and seared through her left arm and shoulder. She half arose but fell back, cried "Oh!" and clutched her arm.

Immediately but almost in a leisurely way, the patients gathered around and looked on her curiously. The nurse pushed through and said, "Y'all sit back down! She's all right, prob'ly a cramp or somethin.'" The mingled voices were louder but still indistinguishable. The woman was not fully conscious but thought of dogs barking after a rabbit farther and farther away.

She did not hear at all when the doctor said, "Two cc's of adrenalin! She may not make it." The nurse gave the shot and he put an oxygen mask on her and listened with the stethoscope. "We had to see too many," he said, feeling the pulse in her right wrist. She turned her hand and grabbed his wrist. He tried to pull away, but she held on. He stroked the back of her hand and said, "Don't worry. We won't let you go."

The pain hit her again and he exclaimed in a kind of wail, "No, honey! Give her more adrenalin. Keep 'er breathin.'" She arched her back and opened and closed her dark eyes and saw him over her. He put the heel of his hand on her sternum, pressed in and gave her mouth to mouth resuscitation. She went limp and he said, "Check the oxygen. Step it up!"

"She's fibrillatin,'" the nurse said.

"Don't die, honey, please!" He was lost in the rhythm of his efforts and in trying to supplant her will with his. With every fourth or fifth push, he said, "Come on!" Shiny with sweat, he worked frenziedly and patted her cheeks and wrists.

After five minutes, the nurse felt the wrist and looked at him. "She's dead," she said. He shook his head and continued. The nurse backed off and watched him for another minute. "She's dead."

"All right!" he conceded, resting his palms on the woman's shoulders and breathing like he had been running.

"What do you want me to do?"

"What?"

"About the patients?"

"Tell 'em to go home. None of 'em are sick anyway."

"I'll call John Green, too."

"I have to get out of here." He left through a vacant office near the outside second story door of Victory Hospital and went down the fire escape to his car.

The nurse covered the woman with a stiff sheet and went into the hallway. "The office'll be closed till two-thirty," she said. "Y'all come back then."

"What happened to the lady?" a little boy asked.

"She had an upset stomach."

The nurse closed the door behind her and one woman said to another, "I don't know why it happened to her. She never went to the doctor."

"They could have seen a few more," a middle-age woman said to a man. "Jackie was next."

"It takes all day to see a doctor around here," the man said. "I'm sorry about the old lady, but I get tired o' waitin'. This little girl's got a sore throat!" he said for the nurse to hear. "Now I got to drive all the way out to the place and back."

"Doctors are still human," said a woman up the hall. "He wouldn't be any good if he didn't care about people dyin'."

"She died," the little boy said. "She saw me makin' faces."

The doctor drove rapidly out of town, squeezing and loosening his hands on the steering wheel, and twelve miles to the country club north of Terkel, Texas. No one was in the bar. He had two drinks and a bacon and tomato sandwich and sat there silently for a long time. He returned at thirty-five miles an hour on the paved farm road coming in on the east side of town.

For the rest of the day, he prescribed shots and cough medicine and gave perfunctory advice until the last patient was gone. He sent the nurse home, sat behind his desk and looked vacantly at the wall. The phone rang and his wife asked, "Darling, are you about through?"

"I'm through."

"Did you have a lot of patients?"

"Depends on how you mean it."

"Come on home. I'll make you feel better."

He locked the doors and went down the stairs to the private parking area behind the hospital. His car stood by itself in a darkening twilight that softened the lines of everything but the car, which stood out hard and shiny. He rubbed his hand along the sharp edge of the fender and said, "Antiseptics and metal symmetrics--fast and beautiful, slow and ugly." The leather seat covers were like perfume. He ran his fingers around the steering wheel, clicking his rings on the notches and putting his hands together at the bottom and top, and smelled the seats, relaxing into them, before starting the engine. "Beautiful," he said. The car floated lightly over crackling rocks and gravel to his home.

Dressed in a long nightgown, his wife met him at the door with a drink in each hand. "Hello, Will," she said, kissing him. "Sit down and relax." They went into the den and she sat across from him on the couch. He smiled at her but did not speak.

"What's the matter?"

"Not too much."

"Come on."

"This old lady had a heart attack at the office and I did the best I could. But she died."

"Who was she?"

"Mrs. Blaine. You may not know her. She took me by the arm to say she wasn't ready. Some people are, you know. We did the right things, but she had another attack and died with me working on her. If you have some warning, you can keep from getting involved. I didn't know her very well because she rarely came in, but she seemed universal like someone good."

"We'll have dinner and you'll feel better."

"I keep feeling her hand on my wrist. I remembered part of a poem about mortality--'a bracelet of bright hair about the bone. . . These miracles we did, but now, alas, all measure and all language I should pass should I tell what a miracle she was.' Wanta go for a drive?"

"Why don't you stay here?"

"Restless."

"I don't think you should go out."

"I'll be back." He was driving away when she came into the yard. He stopped in the street, got out and called, "I'm sorry, Denise. I'll be back in an hour or two. I just need to get out."

"Be careful," she said.

The country club had a dozen cars in the parking lot and an equal number of men standing or sitting around the room. Two brightly dressed golfers were drinking and talking. "No!" one asserted. "You got to use a nine iron from that close."

"Not'n this wind," said the other. "Use a three and hit it low."

Will sat at the bar across from the bartender. "Hi, Doc," the man said. "How you been?" Will didn't answer. "What'll you have? Gin and tonic?"

"Yeah. Been busy?"

"Not so far."

Will looked around occasionally and spoke only if someone spoke to him. After an hour, he started watching the bartender and realized he felt vaguely frightened. The man was big and gave the impression of great power. The bartender saw his expression and asked, "What's the matter, Doc? I'd think a man like you wouldn't have too much to concern him."

"You don't know what you're talking about."

"Maybe not, Doc."

"You don't know anything."

"Maybe not, Doc," the man said, putting his hands on the bar.

"You think you're stronger than me? You're not. I can whip you Indian wrestling."

"Come on, Doc."

"Hey, Jeff won't Indian wrestle me!" Will called.

"Go on, Jeff!" said voices. "Indian wrestle him! I'll bet on you!"

"Naw, naw," said Jeff, smiling and waving his hands as though to cool his legs.

"Come on," Will said, putting his right elbow on the bar with his hand up and fingers open.

The man stood there in discomfiture, looked at the room and said, "Awright." He leaned to the doctor and the others moved around them in a half circle. The mingling voices grew and one said, "You can't."

"Let's go," Will said. He held his hand up with the fingers hooked and rigid. The bartender put his weight onto his elbow and slid it forward until it touched the doctor's. They locked hands and an arm reached in, held them quivering and let go.

Jeff held his arm upright and contemplated Will, who grunted and pushed harder. He moved Jeff back two inches, grinned hysterically and strove with all his strength. "Unh! unh! unh! unh! unh!" he groaned, shoving madly.

Jeff set himself and stopped. He started moving the doctor and brought their hands upright, then gazed up at him and the others as if at dangerous animals.

Will gave way until his arm was halfway down. He saw it descending and fought even harder. Muscles drawn until they looked like bone, he bucked and jerked against Jeff's arm. Veins in his forehead swelled out and sweat sidetracked around them as he hopped and jerked and grunted and bumped the bar with his feet and knees. Tears wetted his bright red face and he cried, "No! no! no! no! no!"

Sweat dripping off his chin, Jeff stared at the back of his hand and shoved. A "pah!" came from Will's elbow and he screamed as it gave way unnaturally. Jeff reached over and moaned, "Aw, man, are you hurt?" Quiet now except for labored breathing, Will sat crookedly on the stool and held his elbow in his left hand.

"He's a doctor," someone said. "You broke his arm."

"You think I meant to?"

"You shoulda known when to quit!" said someone else.

"We ought to take him outside and break his arm," another said.

Will turned as the circle tightened. "You've had all the entertainment you're gettin," he said, putting out his left arm in their direction. "It's only a little bone. I'll be all right." He stood and took Jeff by the shoulder. "Please drive me to the hospital," he said. "I need your help to set this arm."

A GUN AIN'T NO GOOD WITHOUT BULLETS!

Even if you knew they were there, you'd still jerk your hand back and almost fall down the cliff when you felt one. They growled but not loudly. You felt sorry for them, but there was no question of letting one go because they were as dangerous as their owner. There were a half-dozen places where he had attached thick chicken wire over concave places in the rock, detachable on one side. He often had two or three dogs tied down at a time. He came once a day with a water hose, wet them down and squirted water into their mouths. After a day or two, he led them on leashes to the compound where he used them for guard dogs. Combined with the whippings he gave them with a rope kept in a water barrel, the tyings-down and generous feedings made them good dogs, he felt.

He needed them to secure his wrecking yard and the inside of his garage. He had a dozen or so German shepherd and Doberman pinscher-types, liking their biting power and running speed. He put two in the shop at night and the others in the yard, which had a six-foot heavy wire fence. There were no confirmed fatalities, but it was rumored in town that on at least two occasions in the past few years, the dogs had caught a man stealing headlights or a cutting torch or something in the yard. It was said the owner came out of his house and watched with a spotlight but did not intervene. The intruders were buried in the compound and car bodies put over the graves. The men had brought knives and tire tools and killed some of the dogs, but as the owner thought with satisfaction, a pack of dogs can kill almost anything.

I was climbing up the short rock cliff on this night with the expectation of witnessing a murder. I could have gone to the party where it would happen but didn't want to be an official witness. I had long known this man was to be observed only at a distance, if at all, though I knew him and was cordial to him. I even periodically took in minor mechanical work so he would never have cause for resentment. I knew our relationship would not stand my discovery, but there was a thick tree stand on a slope some fifty yards from the party. Under a cloud-cloaked half-moon, I moved to the stand and hunkered down behind a tree trunk to watch the people in the fenced-in basketball court.

The man made people uneasy in our rural West Texas town, but he had a wife and three children under 12 and was apparently never physically abusive to them. He was actually a fine-looking man--six feet tall and one hundred-seventy pounds with brown hair, brown eyes and handsome features. His name was common. He had a hollow way at looking at you, though, and was only pleasant in a lurching fashion, forcing himself to conform to local conventions. No one knew why he was like that. His parents still farmed in the area, a few miles northwest of town. His property had been a small farm that he converted into a junkyard. He didn't bother to grow anything on the unused acreage but kept the weeds and grass down. Some people think the core of the human race is the fallen angels who were cast out of Heaven with Satan. If you believe that, you could say he was one of the darker ones. It seems as good an explanation as any of the duality of human nature and the differences among children in the same families.

As bad men always learn, you can never get so fearsome as to discourage all potential challengers. That's part of what keeps you bad. There is always someone new who has also never been defeated, who believes that when it comes down to the nitty gritty, no one is more formidable than he or she. The fellow who had forced the situation at the party was one of these.

It had started over the price of an engine overhaul. The other man complained loudly that day in the shop that the price was far too high and then carried his complaints to town, calling the man "a crook" and even carrying on about the dogs and rumors of their victims. "Somebody oughta do somethin' about him," he said one morning at the coffee shop. "All that bull! I ain't scared o' him and I ain't payin' him! He can keep the damn motor. I don't need it anyway."

The other man was a farmer who did need the engine to replace one on a well, but it stayed in a corner of the garage as a source of growing annoyance to the mechanic. Mechanics are like plumbers in that they feel the grunginess of their work entitles them to a healthy reward. The unchanging presence of the engine, along with reports of the other man's remarks from friends who hung around the shop, drove the man to a decision he had never expected to make: to kill a man as well-known in the county as he and to do it openly.

The sheriff had never bothered the man except to ask him once if he had any trouble with thieves and to encourage him to ask for help if he ever needed any. The man was an established citizen who did not steal or bother anyone who didn't bother him and in politics you learn not to create any hardcore pockets of opposition unless you absolutely have to. The sheriff knew about the feud and the party, but no laws had yet been broken and there would be plenty of witnesses if anything happened.

The man came into town a couple of times and mentioned he had a birthday coming up and his wife and he were throwing a party. "It don't hurt to be sociable," he said. "We like to be friendly." He came in one morning when he thought his enemy would be in the coffee shop and sat down with him and two other men. "Guess you heard about my party," he said.

"No."

"We're goin' to throw me a birthday party, start bein' little more outgoin' and ever'thang. I know we had that little fuss, but we'd like you an' your wife to come. Nothin' to be afraid of."

"Afraid!" the other man exclaimed. "Afraid o' what?"

"I don' know. You never come picked up y' motor."

"I'll pick it up--and pay what I think it's worth!"

"Awright," the man said, rising and patting the other man on the shoulder. The other man looked angrily at the hand but didn't otherwise move.

"We'll come to y' party," he said. "Be there with bells on."

There was a large crowd, at least for our county. Fifty or sixty people sat at four long tables on the shortened basketball court. There was a meal and the guest of honor began opening his presents. He stood at the head of the table opposite me. His enemy was at the table's other end nearest me with his back to me.

"Well, lookee here!" the man said, taking a big long-barreled revolver from a package. "Guess I could break it in by shootin' ol' Wilbert down there." Grinning, he cocked and aimed it at the other man but then pointed it up.

Wilbert stood and brought a semi-automatic pistol from his coat. "Not if I was you," he said.

The man brought the pistol down and fired, hitting Wilbert around the nose and blowing the back of his head off. Wilbert fell backward over the board seat attached to the table. His feet hit under the table and his legs caught on the seat, bringing him to rest with both legs up, his knees bent and the back top of his head touching the concrete. It looked like he was the only one looking at me--in a macabre way as if to demonstrate he kept some of the athleticism he had had as a youthful gymnast. The other guests dived away, yelling and throwing their arms over their heads. His wife stood there screaming with her arms and fingers thrust out.

"Naw, naw, naw!" the man ejaculated, looking bewildered. "I didn't know it was loaded! Did you load this?" he asked his wife.

"Yes!" she cried. "You always told me a gun ain't no good without bullets!"

I used the pandemonium to get away.

A grand jury ruled that in light of the feud and Wilbert's display of a weapon, the man was justified in reacting defensively. He had told the sheriff that in bringing the pistol down and pulling the trigger, he only meant to show it wasn't loaded. He had planned to laugh and get everyone to laugh with him. His wife said she had loaded it so he would be pleased when he checked it, having always been a man who appreciated a loaded gun.

COACH ARNWINE

J immie Arnwine had been running most of his life and was good enough to get through college on a track scholarship. Running hurdles takes a lot of tenacity and toughness and he had these in abundance. He had dinged himself up plenty of times hitting hurdles and falling but mastered his form and excelled with less talent than many of his teammates and opponents. He was now teaching history and coaching football and basketball as an assistant and track as head coach in a small but oil-rich school in the Texas Panhandle, Destry. All the coaches were in some kind of shape, but Coach Arnwine was in by far the best. Times taper off with age and less intense training and the sixty seconds in which he could still run a quarter-mile would have been slow three years earlier at Hill Top University at Sandstone in Central Texas. But his ability still to do it at twenty-five years old was impressive to everyone.

His running earned respect but not affection because of his vexatious personality. It was a time when coaches were expected to be tough or even a little mean, but he went overboard and seemed to enjoy it, zooming around the track with a paddle and hitting runners he thought were not working hard enough. He'd come up behind them before they knew it, yelling, "Move your ass!" Running so fast, he hit harder than a coach or an administrator could from a standing position. It carried over into the classroom, where he kept his paddle leaning against the desk and used it often, sometimes even on a girl if one were particularly sassy.

Five foot-ten and one hundred-sixty-five pounds with short blond hair and whitish blond eyebrows over perpetually flashing blue-green eyes, he would occasionally just beat the daylights out of a boy and call him back for more if he said anything on the way to his desk. One day he had whipped a smaller boy and then called him back. This one had taken all he could take, staggering as he came to his desk and grabbing it to keep from falling. He did not mean any disobedience but emitted an involuntary exclamation, "Damn!"

Coach Arnwine smiled and crooked his right little finger for the boy to return. "Brewster?" he demanded.

John Crenshaw, the biggest and toughest boy in school, a two hundred-fifty-pounder, got up and moved between them. The coach's plaintive response was odd in retrospect: "But I'm not through yet."

"Yeah, you are," Crenshaw said. The boys sat down and the coach laid the paddle on his desk and resumed teaching.

That was an exception, though. The in-class paddlings and running track zoomings, although somewhat subdued in Crenshaw's presence, continued for another year until a school district fifteen miles away noticed the number of athletes Coach Arnwine took to the state meet and hired him for more money.

Seven times bigger, Terkel was much different than Destry. The students were faster-living and more cynical and the principal stopped him from doing his own paddlings. Zoomings would have been too gauche, so he was reduced to writing reports and trying to get students punished by the principal or head football coach.

Coach Arnwine was by now ten years older than some of the track boys and they thought it funny that he ran with them. He managed to get some swatted, fomenting their antipathy to go with the bemusement. He couldn't stay with the faster ones, but three or four were about his speed. They were having a workout one spring afternoon with a P.E. class, more playing than exerting themselves. He nonetheless had redemptive qualities. He sometimes showed affection for the more dedicated athletes, especially those with few other advantages, and never evinced any racial prejudice.

"Hey, coach, let's you and me and Young and Collins run a quarter for time," a medium-speed boy said. "If you beat us, we'll each give you five dollars. If we beat you, you give each of us five."

"So whoever I beat pays me five and I pay five if anybody beats me?" He had not been working out as much in Terkel as he did in the Destry Dust Devils' more unbridled environment and he knew they were baiting him. The P.E. boys were coming and a crowd was forming. "You three, huh?"

"Just us."

He had grown nearly mad, he felt, with his buttoned-down life and the students' insolence. Unmarried, he was also between checks and needed the money. "Let's go."

Coach Arnwine went to the locker room to put on shorts, track shoes and a purple and gold Terkel Tornadoes T-shirt, came out and slow jogged the cinder circle. The boys stood around laughing until he walked up to them and a group of spectators that had increased to around twenty, including a couple of coaches.

He gave his starter's gun to a coach and got into a crouch. The boys took a standing start because the money was nothing to them and they just wanted to press him. He knew he was not ready to race and wished he hadn't let them sucker him; but he felt the old fury and was enjoying that. These little punks aren't in my class, he thought. They'll never run in college!

He was still in good enough shape to go fast, if not very far, and he burned down the back stretch like a racehorse. It was too fast, but it felt good to be embarrassing them. He could only hear one boy behind him. Yeah, I'll beat them, he thought--use their audience against them!

Face, neck, arms and legs chalky but knees churning furiously and high, he careened into the home stretch. He felt funny, weak, though still flying, in the last fifty yards. The quarter-mile is a taxing distance run close to sprinter's speed. Even top four hundred meter men sometimes collapse, and Coach Arnwine had never been a very good one.

Hurting badly and barely able to breathe, he pushed his body far past the point he should have made it go. All he could see at the finish, with the closest boy two yards behind, was bright white light. The boys laughed when he stumbled roughly to his hands and knees and threw up; then he rolled onto his right side, shuddered and started kicking convulsively with his tongue out and his eyes rolled back. With some yelling and screaming, the teenagers gathered closely around but were scared to touch him. A coach's mouth-to-mouth resuscitation had no effect. An ambulance pulled up and the technicians tried heart paddles. The colloquial story was that his heart had burst, but the truth was that it went into fibrillation and would not come out.

It was disturbing: a young man flying down the track one moment and in his death throes the next. The people in Destry were surprised but not shocked. After a well-attended service in the Terkel High School gymnasium, Coach Arnwine was taken home to Fulcher in Central Texas. His time, fifty-seven-point-two seconds, was repeated each time the story was told. A coach had gotten it precisely in deference to the effort he was making. All the spectators had been transfixed even before he collapsed, watching him run in paler than anyone they had ever seen but with his form unbroken.

THE SPREE KILLER

Paschal County Sheriff Bill Garst was home asleep with his wife, a nurse, and daughters in the next room, dreaming he was a big-time rancher in 1880's Texas. He was riding through tall grass with his cowboys and fat cattle all around. His well-being was so perfect as to be almost liquid as he gave orders and roped calves in the evanescent sphere. Flowing on and on like it would never end, it did with the ringing of his cell phone on the nightstand. Little of urgency happened around Fortner, a town of five thousand, or the ranching, oil-pumping county for Garst's deputies to wake him at two-thirty in the morning; but Deputy Frank Billings said, "Bill, you need to come in. A real bad one is heading our way from Georgia and may be getting close. He stopped an hour ago at Aikins, the other side of Hattonville, and was evidently about to kill a convenience store clerk when the town marshal came in and scared him off without knowing who he was. He's killed four people in his hometown and at a convenience store outside Tuscaloosa, Alabama."

Garst's mind was churning as he got up, told his wife he had an emergency, put on his Wrangler jeans, cowboy shirt, boots, hat and holster and took his .40-caliber semi-automatic pistol off the top shelf in the closet. "What's going on, Bill?" his wife Cindy asked.

Too many cops keep their families in the dark, which is part of the reason so many get divorced, he had long thought. "There's a fugitive coming west down I-20. He may have already gotten past us, but if we catch him we will handle him."

"What do y'all call it, the sewer line of America?"

"That's it."

"Don't take any chances."

"Don't worry, we won't."

He went to the highway to park behind an abandoned mobile home manufacturer's building and watch. Billings had run the road east from Fortner past Williford, one of the county's two smaller towns, to look for the green Ford Crown Victoria that Aaron Burns had stolen from a salesman he killed at Tuscaloosa. The sheriff did not yet see the need to call out all four deputies because Burns had been through Aikins about twelve forty-five and could have covered the hundred-twenty miles through Paschal County by now. The county also had the town of Stautner on the west. Both Stautner and Williford had state rest stops nearby and Garst called the deputy who usually worked in the Williford area, Homero Feliz, to join Billings there.

He dialed up the report on the computer in his car and the more he read, the more disturbed he got. Burns was a black man in his late twenties who had done three years in Dooly State Prison at Unadilla, Ga., for turning off the refrigeration at a supermarket in his hometown of Copperdale and ruining ten thousand dollars of meat. At five foot eight and a hundred twenty-five pounds, he probably had a tough go in the pen. Working as a waiter after his parole, within a few months he took a prostitute into the woods and killed her with a knife, possibly for practice, investigators speculated. Burns got into a fracas with some friends at the restaurant, chased them outside and shot a man in the back of the head with a twelve-gauge pump shotgun as they tried to drive away, shooting big lead slugs like some hunters use to kill deer with at close range.

Burns fled Copperdale and hid in Atlanta for a couple of weeks until turning up at Tuscaloosa, where he stopped at the gasoline pumps in his compact car, went inside to look around about midnight and came back with the shotgun. He shot the clerk, a popular Vietnam veteran, then dropped the salesman between the restroom and front door. Burns rifled the cash register, bagged food and drinks and took the salesman's wallet, cell phone, credit cards and car. Leaving the store, he held up his right index finger to the camera to signify "No. 1." On the way to Texas, he called his former high school teachers and others, bragging that he would be soon be on America's Most Wanted.

Reading all this, Garst understood that Burns might be the first man he would have to kill. As a deputy in a neighboring county, he had once fired his pistol into the ceiling to persuade a wife-beater to put down a rifle. He had never shot anyone but started planning how it should be done. He decided to have Feliz do it because killing a black man would be less subject to controversy if a Mexican-American did it. Watching the traffic go by, he knew that unless this man surrendered, he would have to be shot to protect the officers and public.

Blond, balding and not a big man, Garst waited in the median until four a.m., certain such a car as the salesman's had not passed. It had been more than three hours since Burns left Aikins, surely continuing west, so he must have beaten the stakeout. Feliz and Billings said he hadn't come through Williford and was not in that rest stop, so it appeared he had gotten through Paschal County and was now someone else's concern. Cops were watching from there to El Paso, so there was little chance he would avoid capture. Getting on his radio, the sheriff told the deputies, "Looks like he got past us. I'm going to Stautner before we pack it in. It'd be a fluke if he was there."

Garst thought the night was over as he drove into the rest stop west of Stautner and started past the cars, pickups, vans and SUVs. He was normally quite nervy and seldom felt fear, but when he saw a green Ford with the salesman's South Carolina license plate on the right near the restroom building, he had a sensation unlike any he had known--the weight of life and death with death clammy and close. He kept going to the end of the area and stopped on the roadside with his lights off. Having monitored the car in his mirrors, he turned around in the seat to be doubly certain nothing had moved.

Garst picked up his radio and said with his voice shaking a little, "Homero and Frank, get all the deputies up and call the highway patrol. I believe I have found the suspect asleep in the Stautner rest stop. Get here as fast as you reasonably can, but approach slowly and be very quiet. We have to get all these people out of here before approaching the suspect because there could be shooting. I'll park near the east entrance and wait for you. Do you read me?" Opening his windows to listen, he heard the busy creaking of a pump jack in the adjacent pasture. A soft dry breeze soughed through the grass and mesquites, and he was dismayed to find himself wishing it would rain.

Feliz, twenty-five miles away, did over a hundred miles an hour while Billings hit eighty and ninety. The tricky part was moving among the vehicles, waking people up without alerting Burns and having them start their engines, drive out and keep going. The other two deputies and two highway patrolmen joined in the half-hour operation. Then with the rest area cleared of everyone but the cops and killer, Texas Highway Patrolman

Carlos Armendariz put spikes in front of the Ford's front and back tires. Garst stationed Feliz behind the car with a military rifle and instructions to shoot to kill if the engine started. Garst thought it was funny later, but no one saw the humor when he clicked on his bullhorn and called twice, "Aaron Burr, come out of the car with your hands up!"

Burns peeked over the front seat and, keeping his head low, started the car. Feliz had planned to shoot through the back windshield and seat, but when the car lurched over the spikes with a "pah-pah-pah-pah!" as the tires deflated and shot over the curb and across the lawn, the coldbloodedness of the occasion kept him from doing so and he just fired warning shots through the right side of the glass and into the air. Broad-shouldered and muscular, Homero was a genial family man who had the reputation of handling emergencies quickly and decisively. He had lots of moxie and had been in innumerable scrapes, but he had never killed a man and found himself unable to here.

Burns clattered away as fast as the car would go and onto the highway just as the sun was coming up with the cops strung out behind with their lights and sirens. He drew even with Dillon Cauthon of Fortner, who was on his way to work on a drilling rig and had slowed in obeisance to the brilliant, cacophonous approach of the law enforcement caravan. Burns looked at Cauthon with a lost expression of rage and rammed the side of the pickup truck. Cauthon sped up and dodged away to escape having his door collapsed as the killer went into a sidelong skid ending with the car turned onto its right side. Garst ran, jumped up and reached in to keep Burns away from the shotgun. Then Feliz, Billings and the others helped pull him out to be handcuffed on the gravelly shoulder of the road.

Later pondering what had gone right and wrong, the sheriff thought he should have given the kill shot to one of the highway patrolmen because they're specifically trained to use deadly force if necessary. He wouldn't reprimand Feliz because his record had been excellent, but he sharply regretted the danger Cauthon had been exposed to and the damage to his pickup.

The attorney general of Georgia sent an airplane with two big cops and an empty seat for Burns, who would be tried and imprisoned in Georgia and then in Alabama if he avoided the death penalty and was ever released. Garst was interviewed by the editor of the Fortner Echo, who watched Burns' transfer of custody and shouted as he was led outside, "What went wrong, Aaron?" There was a glance but no response. Garst followed the van twenty-five miles to High Gate Airport and watched the plane till it disappeared.

Feliz accepted the joking by other deputies about his marksmanship in good spirits, but the police chief's job opened in the small town of Bearheart in a neighboring county and he took it. He was working the night shift alone two years later when he stopped a dark gray van with Missouri license plates. It was misting at three a.m. on what had been a dull February night when he clocked the van going fifteen miles over the thirty-five-mph limit.

In a vulnerable position walking up on the driver's side, he was somehow not surprised when a tall young white man in a black hoodie elbowed the door open and stepped out aiming a heavy pistol. Feliz drew his .45-caliber semi-automatic cleanly and they leveled at each other and emptied their magazines from a distance of twenty-five feet. Both were accurate, putting most of their bullets into the other man; but Homero was a little better, starting in the body and working up to the neck while all the other man's fire went into his bullet-proof vest except for two that hit his left arm and lower left leg. The dead man was with two women and a younger man who obeyed Homero's order to sit by the road with their hands behind their heads.

Many people resent the police because of the prospect of getting a ticket and cops wonder if anyone appreciates the risks they take. The truth is that cops are liked or disliked, especially in small towns, for the same reasons everyone else is. Homero learned he was well liked by just about everyone who knew him and admired by many who did not. His photo in bed at High Gate Hospital among cards and flowers from fifteen or twenty counties was published in the regional Hattonville Cryer-Times and he got scores of calls and visits from officers and citizens, most of whom imagined themselves in the predicament he had faced and figured they would have died. One who visited was Bill Garst.

"I don't have any broken bones, luckily," Homero said. "The doctors say I won't be disabled after I rehabilitate."

"I think this is a little ironic after our arrest of the spree killer," said Garst. "You ended up forced into it and handled yourself extremely well."

"I fought for my life and was lucky enough to survive. I still don't think I could do it cold, even now."

"That's to your credit. Some business we're in, huh?"

"Does it make any sense?"

"Not a whole lot."

And they laughed.

THE PURITY OF JAZZ
AND SPECKLED TROUT

This marriage is ridiculous, thought Angel, looking at her husband asleep on the couch. A radio disc jockey in Baton Rouge, she had been proud of Raymond's status as an attorney in the early years, hosting fish fries in the backyard of their home forty miles southeast of town, until realizing he had inherited more than a name from his late grandfather, Governor Ernest "Lucky" Leakey (pronounced Lakey), whose unofficial motto had been, "The oath of office is not a vow of poverty." Most of their friends were from the political crowd in the capitol--lobbyists, legislators and contractors involved in bid-rigging on state projects like highways and hospitals. There were women at the parties, and Angel could tell Ray knew some of them in the wrong way. He was a tall, pudgy man with black hair parted down the middle and a thick neck. His characteristic expression these days was mild indignation, but he was passed out and snoring now in polka dot boxer shorts with his belly fat stuck to the purple Naugahyde couch. He had taken up cocaine with some of his more dissolute friends, and Angel was sure he would end up being disbarred. The Nauga Doll on the coffee table was laughing.

She put on Nat King Cole's "Unforgettable," made a Crown and Coke and lit a Marlboro, trying to relax and clear her mind. It was summertime and the sliding glass back door was open. She had been so preoccupied that she hadn't noticed the splashing of the speckled trout. It was their breeding season and they were going nuts. She had become adept at fishing and enjoyed it, although cleaning the catch was always Ray's chore.

It was two a.m. Sunday. She changed into her fishing togs and walked into the moist night air with her rod and tackle box. Good equipment was necessary because speckled trout, silver-sided with olive green backs and little black dots, were lively and strong at three or four pounds. Live bait was good, but Angel had found the tandem rigged artificial split-tail beetle lures effective and easier to handle.

Leaving their power boat, she rowed the dinghy a couple of hundred yards into the salt water inlet from Lake Ponchartrain. The fish, also known as spotted sea trout, started hitting her line and worked the change she wanted, shoving the booze and cigarette smoke, drunken laughter and knowing floozies, sotted cronies and semi-secret cocaine snorting to the back of her mind as the trout tested her will and the muscles in her arms, back and shoulders.. It was exhilarating to feel that tug, set the hook, crank the reel, fight the fish until it was close, guide it into the net and drop it flopping into the boat. Trout after trout after trout were the needed beguilement. Whipping her line out, she thought of the "Bill Dance Outdoors" cable show and guests of the sunglasses-wearing host like country music stars Mel Tillis and Hank Williams Jr.

Married for six years now, she had fallen in love with Ray when he was a parish prosecutor, effervescent and witty. She found him fascinating because no matter what the question, he instantly had the answer, well-framed and complete. Angel was a country girl from Plaquemine, a child of schoolteachers, her father a coach and her mother a music teacher who had taught her piano. Angel taught music in a junior high but was drawn to radio and found a gift for it. What she liked about jazz, working from ten p.m. to three a.m. Tuesday through Friday on WBRG, was its vividness and purity. She played the contemporary stuff, but the essence of her appeal as the raspy-voiced Angel Jeansonne was her reliance on classics like Billie Holiday's live cut of "I Cover the Waterfront," with which she closed each show.

The law and politics were Ray's milieu by birthright and inclination, and she had seen there were advantages to being Lucky Leakey's grandson because there were lots of people around the capitol who had known the governor, Louisiana's first to be imprisoned after a scandal involving thefts and frauds. They still thought fondly of the elder Leakey as a Huey Long protege and embraced his grandson as a legatee of the Kingfish tradition. Ray loved it, sometimes remarking, "Granddaddy bent a few rules, but he never mistreated his friends." He was a mid-level criminal defense lawyer whose legitimate work slowed when he stopped taking appointments to concentrate on lobbying for the contractors and trying to keep them from being indicted. He still represented a few defendants and did wills, contracts and probate work, but his undisciplined lifestyle was gradually dragging him down.

After three hours of more intense fishing than she had ever done, Angel quit because her arms hurt too much. The dinghy was not particularly small or she would stopped sooner because she had around a hundred fish. The boat sat low in the water and she rowed carefully back. They had plenty of ice in an outdoor freezer, and she packed the kitchen sink, bathtub and some coolers before carrying the fish in on stringers. Ray was still on the couch. He came here on most nights, but Angel often stayed at their city apartment. She loaded clothes, shoes and toiletries into her two-tone blue Mercury Cougar and left a note by the Nauga Doll, a little brown monster with horns and jagged yellow teeth, saying, "I'm sorry, but I don't like living like this."

TOM FALLON

The scent of cut grass in the soft south breeze in the Victory Broncos' grandstands was evocative when the Class of 1965 was called to the fifty yard line. To the old players, it meant August practices, September, October and November games, swift opponents, hard hits, dejection and elation. It was their thirtieth anniversary and the unveiling of the bust of Tom Fallon, who would have graduated in '64 had he not died the previous summer. He was mostly forgotten until alumni petitioned the school board to rename Broncos' Field for him and raised seventy five hundred dollars for the bust.

Although he was remembered primarily as a track star, the ceremony was appropriate because track in the '60's was really about football--to improve team speed. Fallon's sixty-yard interception return during his junior season was recounted by his classmate Wes Wilson, as were his broken right forearm, inability to play basketball and wintertime running to set the school record, still standing, of forty nine point five seconds in the four hundred meters. English teacher Frankie Rivers read "Sailing to Byzantium:" "Once out of nature, I shall never take My bodily form from any natural thing, But such a form as Grecian goldsmiths make Of hammered gold and gold enamelling. . ." Fallon's parents, Frank and Donna, accepted a wreath and his sister Regina said, "Tom loved being a Bronco and was a true example of the Broncos' spirit."

Johnny Whitechapel remembered Tom's interception from the following Monday's film review and mused on the last time he saw him, a summer afternoon the week before a tractor turned over on him as he crossed a ditch northwest of town. His father dug him from under the tractor and drove him to Victory Hospital in the front seat of his pickup truck. Johnny recalled the day when he and two friends went to the field. They were leaving the dressing room when Johnny opened the training room door and there was Tom with a vacant look on his freckled, sweating face and eyes. They assumed he had heard them coming and hidden, uncomfortable with boys from a different class, and they laughed and looked oddly at one another outside as they left.

Tom was a good pass catching end and defensive back, but Johnny thought more about the running. An average half miler who enjoyed the meets, Johnny watched the relay teams practice all season on the graded dirt track. With a smooth style like a waterfall, Wilson was the second fastest. Max Cornell was a fullback who could run a ten flat hundred yard dash, high jump six feet, dunk a basketball and put the shot almost fifty feet. Max consistently ran under fifty three seconds. Charlie Ralston played the unusual combination of quarterback and linebacker and ran flat out over the whole four hundred-forty yards of the mile relay. He broke fifty six on pure guts, handing off to Wes for the third leg as white as porcelain. They won all the way to the Texas state meet and finished second. Tom would win the quarter mile and anchor the relay, flashing down the back stretch, lengthening the lead, his red silk uniform's crinkling in the sun. He had run outside during basketball season and would come into the gym and run the stands with leather sandbags on his ankles and ice on his cheeks and eyebrows.

Each player's experience of a practice, game or season is different. There are friends, rivals and enemies among thirty or forty boys, but they all felt a discomfiture when Coach Todd Newton put Fallon's jersey, No. 88, on a hanger in the ceiling of the dressing room. No one said anything until Ralston asked Newton on the second day of practice to take it down. "I can't take it," said Charlie, hanging his head.

The freshmen did not easily gain admittance to the elite society. Some were more readily accepted, those who would make the A team as sophomores, but for most it was a daily initiation entailing cheap shots in practice, athletic balm in jockey straps and other harassments. Johnny did not like the drills but came to enjoy the scrimmages, playing on and on in the heat and dust, and the games they won. He sometimes thought they should play every day forever, starting in the morning, breaking for lunch and supper and sleeping on the field until it was time to resume.

The season before Tom died, they were ninth in the Texas State Class 1-A rankings after the first three games but faded and ended six and four. They played with a vengeance the next year and clobbered their top rival in the ninth game to go into the last one unbeaten. The offense was flat and it was zero-zero in the last minute, when Coach Newton thought the Blackwater Buffaloes had more penetrations and told the strong-armed B team quarterback to throw four long passes that failed. The defense played well, but the Buffaloes had an elite halfback, Ricky Feller, and starting from the twenty five yard line ran four plays and scored. Victory still won a co-district championship trophy, but Newton lost the coin flip to make the playoffs. Having led by three penetrations to two inside the twenty yard line and needing only to punt and rely on Charlie and the defense, Newton was fired and a new coach took the team to the championship the next year.

Johnny was living in Victory the summer of the thirty year reunion and often went running, thinking about the old relay team and trying to use good form. One day in the post office, Frank Fallon grinned sideways at him from under the bill of his oily red cap and said, "I saw you runnin' yesterday. You looked good!"

MELODY MOREHOUSE

Perhaps because a musician's life may embrace strange or painfully amusing contrasts, Billy John Harlow was singing the best and living the worst that he ever had in his life. Battered by his second divorce and doing poorly at his day job, selling used cars at the far south end of Texton's main drag, he couldn't afford a band and lately had been limited to sitting in with friendly bandleaders who'd let him do a few songs. Luke Jackson and the Get Down Country Bluesboys were playing the Whistlestop Club on North College Avenue. It had been a hot day and was still warm outside at ten o'clock when Billy John walked in. There were a dozen people sitting around, dancing and drinking at the bar. Luke and a couple of musicians waved or nodded as he sat down and the barmaid brought a can of Miller Light. One of the couples dancing under the sparkling disco ball wore matching clothes--tight, faded jeans, blue striped shirts, silver western buckles and black lizard cowboy boots. They two-stepped, moved back and whirled in a complex pattern Billy John had not seen before. They were so good as to be mesmerizing. The man looked serene and the woman troubled.

Billy John didn't notice Melody Morehouse until Luke finished the set and sat at a table with her, beckoning him to join them. It had been over twenty years since he last saw her in

Victory, Texas, a small farm town fifty miles southwest of Texton. The last he had heard of Melody, the beer can-dragging, ribald slogan-smeared Oldsmobile her husband and she had taken on their honeymoon to Dallas was broken into and robbed. Her father Norman, a prominent cotton farmer and decorated World War II Army veteran, was a smallish, emotional man whose earnest expression his daughter still reflected. She had been an "all-everything" girl--cheerleader, high-stepping drum major, basketball player, track sprinter and of course high-toned date.

Sitting there talking with Luke and her after their mutual mild surprise and acknowledgement, Billy John began thinking of her erstwhile love affair with Max Cornell, a star football player turned rodeo cowboy. Billy John had gone through a cowboy phase and run around with Max, who was two years older, breaking wild horses and going to rodeos and rodeo dances with Max and some friends. One night when they got into Max's new yellow Dodge Charger, they were intrigued to see lever-action deer rifles hanging on padded metal hooks on the lower inside of each door. Max said he had been feeding his horses just off a dirt road east of Victory when somebody started shooting at him. He had fallen onto the ground and crawled under the tin-roofed shed until the shooting with something big like a .30/06 stopped after ten or twelve shots that smacked into the fence posts and shed walls. Max still had the rifles on his doors when he left to work on a ranch near Abilene the next year.

As Luke and Billy John talked about the music business, he saw Melody looking oddly at him and wondered if she was thinking about that period, too, because Max thought it was her daddy warning him to stay away from her. Considering the effort Mr. Morehouse had made to give Melody advantages, Billy John figured Max was right. The relationship was not as serious as Morehouse feared, so Max stopped asking her out. Billy John had not known if he told her why, but he thought now, sitting with Luke and her, that she had become aware at some point. "I haven't seen you in forever, Billy John," she said. "How are you doing?"

"Not so great," he said. "I did okay for awhile. I'm way down deep in the valley."

"I can't wait to hear you," she said, winking. She still had that West Texas girl look like a brunette Tanya Tucker. They didn't have much to talk about because she had been three grades ahead of him.

Admired in Victory during his years as a powerful, speedy fullback and all-around track athlete, Max Cornell had become somewhat controversial since then, hanging around town and becoming fairly successful as a saddle bronc rider; but Billy John and his friends knew he was not a bad guy-- fun-loving and sometimes rowdy but not dangerous or self- destructive. Billy John didn't know anything about Melody's ex-husband or what he had done for a living, but he thought she might have been happier with Max, who had gotten fat, stayed married and become manager of a big ranch's registered cattle herd after studying genetics for a year at Northeast Texas Agricultural Science College.

Luke Jackson was a pretty good guy and probably the best country singer in Texton, a city of two hundred thousand. Owning a paint and body shop, he was in good enough financial shape to push his music aggressively, going to Nashville once or twice a year and making one record after another. He was also known for having the best marijuana in town, though he seldom showed the effects. He was a big, friendly guy with a huge bass voice that he used to terrific effect on songs like Hoyt Axton's "Evangelina" and Cal Smith's "Hello, Country Bumpkin."

"I'll do a couple and call you up," he said. "Do five or six if you want to. I can use the rest."

Luke returned to the bandstand, opening with his new single. "I'm gettin' rubbed the wrong way by the calloused hands of time," he sang, grinning and shaking his head. "That old grandfather clock, you know, he ain't no friend of mine." He did Hank Thompson's "Blackboard of My Heart" and Jim Reeves' "Welcome to My World," introduced Billy John to applause from no one but Melody and handed Billy John his red Rickenbacker guitar.

Billy John didn't usually think about much on stage except the music, but that night, singing Randy Travis's "On the Other Hand," he thought of how an songwriter's work is based on everything that happens to him. His mind was a kaleidoscope of action, images and conversations from the past as he glanced at Luke and Melody, who watched with wholly disparate expressions.

THE FIRE IN THE GARDEN

Chief of Police Tag Tankersley of the City of Jimmerson on the Texas High Plains was dozing but not asleep. He had been dreaming about his late mother, how he had not always been pleased when she called but that he wished she could call him now to end with "I love you" again. His wife Nadine lay with him under the sheet with a ceiling fan tick-tick-ticking. It was a spring night, three a.m., in the early 1950's. Their yellow and brown two-story home shone dully in the full moonlight and the streetlight on the corner. The phone rang and he rolled over quickly because Nadine could get cranky when waked from a sound sleep. So he had the tension of responding appropriately while minimally disturbing her. "Chief Tankersley?" a woman asked.

"Yes, m'am?" he answered.

"This is Faye Norris. A man was just in my bedroom."

"How'd he get in?"

"Through my second-story window."

"Did you know him?"

"I couldn't tell, didn't have my glasses on."

"Is he gone?"

"He went out through the window."

"Does your bedroom door lock?"

"Yes."

"Get up and lock the window and door, turn on your bedroom light and wait for us. Me'n' Nadine'll be right there."

Nadine did not mind getting up when he explained. The culprit looked to be absent when they reached the Norris house in Tankersley's black Buick with the toothy grill and "Jimmerson Police Department" in white lettering on the sides. Faye was a widow of good reputation in her early 70's who, he admitted to himself, was one of the better-looking elderly women in the town of four thousand. Her husband had been a prosperous farmer and she lived in a big two-story brick house that was often the Sunday setting of Order of the Eastern Star meetings. This is a major crime, Tag thought, rumbling through the moonlight and shadows while Jimmerson slept. "Good Lord!" he exclaimed. "Faye Norris! We'll have to take her to the hospital."

The upper bedroom light was on and he stopped in the street where she could see him and tapped the horn. She came down, wearing a black dress and shoes, to let them in, big-eyed behind thick wire-rimmed glasses. After Tankersley, carrying a flashlight, checked each room and the backyard, they sat in the living room like it was a social call. Faye had been crying but had powdered her face and was trying to compose herself.

She looked to Nadine first and then to Tag, saying, "I'll tell you what happened. I woke up and he was on top of me. He held my arms down and just did it. I was so scared, I couldn't move or say anything. He got up and pulled up his pants and went back out the window. I think I heard him jump to the ground."

"Did he holler like he was hurt?"

"No. He was medium-height and kind of wiry, not fat at all. He didn't really stink, but he smelled gamey like he'd been in the woods."

Tag thought that was a little odd because there were no woods nearby, only flat farmland, scattered tree groves and some ranchland and sandhills. "Do you have any idea who it was?"

"Well, Ronnie Carroll comes to mind, but I'd hate to falsely accuse him."

Her mention of Carroll seemed credible in one way and questionable in another. The mentally handicapped brother of a one-time star high school basketball player who was now a moderately successful farmer, Ronnie had been suspected in a few petty break-ins and thefts of change at businesses but had never done anything like this. He was in his mid-to late 30's. His family looked after him some, providing a house that bordered on a shack where he lived with dogs and sometimes goats. His oft-expressed ambition to anyone who would listen around the service stations and other places was to become a long-haul trucker. It was possible, Tag supposed, that in his yearning to be like other men, he had roamed the town at night, spying on ladies and eventually targeting one. "I wouldn't say this if Nadine wasn't here, but he did say something that I guess you should know about," said Mrs. Norris.

"What?"

"While he was holding me down, he said somethin' strange four or five times."

"What was it?"

"Sexpot."

The word half-chilled, half-amused the chief, but he stayed poker-faced. He called a doctor and took Mrs. Norris, with his wife, to the hospital to have her examined and get a semen sample. The rapist's blood type was O Positive, the most common, which could eliminate Carroll but not incriminate him.

They didn't try to cover it up except to persuade the newspaper editor not to report it, for decency's sake, because they knew it would get around anyway. Certainly, the ladies started locking up at night. Ronnie Carroll was a subject of suspicion but not the only one. Although some men get meaner with age, there were a number of citizens who, like Chief Tankersley, considered Carroll relatively harmless. People liked him or had compassion for him and didn't want him treated unjustly.

Ronnie was not afraid of Tankersley unless he had done something, when, of course, he was easily read. Tag found him sitting on a curb downtown, drinking a red soda pop. Ronnie looked nervous but was doing a fair job of disguising it, taking a swig and looking around casually like he hadn't seen Tag coming.

"Hi, Ronnie!" Tag called.

"Hi, Chief!" he answered, friendly as always.

"What're you doin' here?"

Ronnie blushed and said, "Nothin.'"

"You need to come to the hospital with me."

"What for?"

"Stick your finger."

"Naw, Chief!"

"Come on, Ronnie, it won't hurt much. I'll buy you another soda pop."

Tankersley, a big fellow in his mid-forties, got Ronnie up and walked him to the car. He felt sorry for Ronnie and liked his family, but he couldn't dilly-dally around because the word was getting out and he couldn't chance another rape. They passed the Delphi Theater, where a Jane Russell-Robert Mitchum movie, "His Kind of Woman," was playing. He asked, "Whaddaya call a real pretty woman?"

"Purty."

"What if she's real purty?"

"Sexpot."

"Where'd you hear that word?"

"I don't know, picture show."

"Know what happens when you make me mad?"

"I ain't gunna."

"Put you in jail and the prisoners get you."

"Whadda'll they do?"

"They whup you all the time, get you naked and make you cry ever' night. That's what happens when you do somethin' bad to a lady and she tells me. Miz Norris told me somebody done somethin' bad to her. Was it you?" He stared at Ronnie like he had never done before, having stopped in the hospital parking lot.

"Naw, Chief, I didn't!"

"I know you did, but I'm gonna wait three days to throw you in jail with the mean men."

Ronnie was really scared and Tag had to handcuff him and walk him into the hospital. He sobbed when the nurse stuck his finger, but Tag felt a surge of hope. He would have gladly told Ronnie he was joking and couldn't he take a joke and would have bought him three red soda pops and a big bag of peanuts and told him to forget it, he wasn't going to jail after all, if only the blood test proved him wrong. But they waited in adjacent chairs in the hall until the nurse reported the sample and it was O Positive.

"Remember, Ronnie, I'm gonna wait three days to put you in jail with the mean men," Tankersley said in the car. "But we're gonna be watchin' you day and night, so don't get in no more ladies' houses! Understand?" He pulled his .44-caliber revolver and put it in Ronnie's face to. "If you do, I'll shoot you! Understand?"

Ronnie knocked open the door and ran, flailing his arms and sobbing. Tag found it repugnant, but his duty to protect the citizenry was at times unpleasant. If you don't have the stomach for the job, he often thought, you shouldn't take it on. He was hoping Ronnie would hang himself or jump off the water tower or something, leaving everyone to draw their own conclusions and saving the spectacle and expense of court, not to mention the possibility of an acquittal with the victim's poor eyesight and the pervasiveness of Type O blood. Considering the publicity associated with Jane Russell movies, the "sexpot" reference was conclusive in his mind; but he could hear a lawyer hired by the Carrolls tearing it to pieces, making a joke of it and spawning a law enforcement nightmare with Ronnie still loose on the town.

Tag and his three officers kept up with Ronnie but rode a loose herd. Ronnie went out some at night but didn't wander or try to elude them, although he was furtive, scurrying at times and looking over his shoulders. In the late afternoon of the third day, the Tankersleys were home, eating pork chops, spinach, mashed potatoes and corn. The phone rang and Patrolman Arlis Duesler said, "We're at Ronnie's."

"What happened?" Tag asked.

"You remember how he always got gas to burn off his garden?"

"Yeah."

"It ain't too pretty."

Rosser County Justice of the Peace Sam Silver, a woman, was there with Duesler, a mortician and a couple of neighbors. The garden was burned off and so was Ronnie. He lay on his side like he had toppled over and all his clothes and skin were gone. He was cooked a light red and a peculiarly sweet scent hung in the cool, moist air. Tag picked up a five-gallon gasoline can six feet in front of Ronnie to reveal the can-size circle of grass and weeds that were the only unburned things in the garden. Texas JP's can be independent and he was glad to be on good terms with Sam, tentatively venturing, "Does it look to you like an accident?"

Judge Silver looked at him shrewdly and said, "Could be. They said he filled that can and walked a good half-mile with it. I don't see a cap, so it prob'ly splashed all over his pant legs."

"He sloshed it around the garden, got even more on him, lit a match and Katy, bar the door," Tankersley said, pushing up the brim of his white cowboy hat.

"I'll rule accidental death. Didn't have a reason to do away with hisself, did he?"

"Don't think so. I think ol' Ronnie was always purty happy, didn't know no better. Prob'ly didn't suffer much 'cause he couldn't breathe."

"Be less embarrassin' for the fam'ly," the judge said.

"Yeah, and if he had anything on his conscience, he don't now."

Gruesome as it was, it took a big weight off the chief. He had left his supper half-eaten and Nadine got the plate out of the oven. The pork chops were succulent. He smelled them, cut a piece, put it into his mouth and chewed it. But the smell from the garden was still in his nostrils. He swallowed and realized the competing scents were radically incongruent and that the juiciness of the meat was revolting. He tried a bite of spinach and that didn't work, either. "Guess I lost my appetite," he said, pushing his chair back to get up. "Somethin' on the job."

Nauseous, he weaved through the living room and front door and sat in the porch swing. Nadine came out and sat with him.

"Tough stuff, huh, buddy?" she asked.

"Yeah," he said, thinking he would wait a couple of days for the story about the fire to get around and go see Faye Norris. She had merely wanted to see the rapist in jail, he knew, but he would tell her why he was sure it was Ronnie and explain that it was better to avoid a trial. He would tell her Ronnie couldn't live with himself, knowing that when she had thought it over, the outcome would be satisfactory.

THE BAD TEDDY

Y ou are not insane, at least no more than many people in their imaginations. They fantasize about doing things like you did, though not for the same reasons. For a long time, you had been increasingly distressed that some license plates were wonderful, some pretty good, some so-so, some bad and a few very bad. The very bad are the ones you finally decided to take emphatic action against and not just the bad plates but also the people who had them on their cars, pickup trucks, tractor-trailer rigs and sport utility vehicles. It might theoretically be possible to be a good person and have a bad license plate, but you felt and knew that they would not be displaying those plates if they did not agree with them.

You live in a two-story house less than a mile from Loop 492 on the west side of Texton, which is a city of about two hundred thousand in West Texas. You're on the south side of a four-lane divided highway known as Rondale Road because it leads to Rondale, New Mexico, one hundred-twenty miles west.

Your identity is as yet unknown. The police and others think you are a gun nut of some stripe, but they're wrong. You only have one gun, but it is a good one, a Bushmaster AR-15 223-caliber assault rifle. The original models were used by American soldiers in Vietnam, and they have been improved a good deal since then. You are not a former soldier or a hunter, but you have practiced with your AR a lot and are quite good with it. Your parents owned a big cotton farm with oil wells and left you so much money that you don't have to work, although you went to Texton University and took a degree in sociology. You've been diagnosed as having schizotypal syndrome, but that doesn't mean you are schizophrenic, just that you do not relate well to people and may develop peculiar ideas.

Having been religious with idealistic tendencies, you stopped attending church as a young adult and developed an interest in numerology that became an obsession. You read numerology books and began interpreting every set of numbers you saw without considering the sinister aspects that were becoming more prominent. You started noticing untoward numbers and letters on license plates on Loop 492 and would have said every tenth or twelfth vehicle had one of the bad or very bad kinds. Here are a couple of examples. A white Chevrolet pickup had KUS-7080. That's "CUSS" or "SUCK" with seven plus eight making fifteen, meaning six and the Devil. An old blue Lincoln had ADB-8122, meaning "BAD-13." The import is obvious. On the good side, a red Toyota Camry had KYS-4111, meaning "KISS" or "SKY-7," an excellent message, and a black Chrysler New Yorker had AAB-2205, or "BAA-9," meaning the sheep want something different, and you can't blame them for that.

It was exhilarating, by far the most stimulating thing you had ever done. You have two pickups, a new red one and an older black one that still ran well. You made mud to obscure the license plates, which had good messages on both vehicles. They had tried to give you some so-so ones at the Texton County Tax Assessor's Office, but you made them keep getting others until they proffered some you liked. You put your AR-15 in the black pickup with the butt up and the muzzle in the floorboard, drove to the Loop and started around it, going south on the outside. You didn't see any bad plates for awhile and were thinking all the people with bad plates had been warned. Then a blue Ford F-150 passed, going fast. His plate was "STZ-9601," or "ZTS-16," making fun of you because you had had acne as a teenager.

You gunned it, came up to his left rear and fired five shots into that part of the pickup. He looked around wild-eyed, and you fired twice more to show him what was happening. He jerked his steering wheel hard right and ran off the Loop and through the grass to the access road. He may have been diddling someone's wife or have owed money to a loan shark, but he got the idea in a hurry. You cut across the median, got going the other way and made it home in a few minutes, putting the black pickup into your two-vehicle garage and leaving the red one outside. The sirens began soon after you made it inside, and you admit to having enjoyed the TV news and were looking forward to seeing the Texton Ledger in the morning.

It was getting so sensational, being on all three TV stations and in the Ledger each day, that you decided to get off the Loop for awhile. You drove up Rondale Road in the late afternoon for a new target, something different, because the city cops were all over the Loop. You had them so fired up that you knew they would shoot to kill if they caught you running, even though nobody had been hit except for a pickup driver who caught a bullet fragment in the calf of one leg above his boot.

You'd gone up Rondale Road about twenty-five miles when an eighteen-wheeler hauling cattle tail-gated you really closely and then turned wildly into the passing lane, sloshing urine and feces over the side of the trailer. This truck really stank, and the plate read, "HTT-4621," which could have been interpreted "HOT-13" or "HATE-13." It doesn't necessarily stop a truck to shoot the outside dual tire, so you came up and shot the left front tire by the driver, who was a skinny cowboy with whiskers and tobacco stains on his cheeks. You appreciated that driving a cattle truck is not the best trucking job, but there is a good way and a bad way to do anything, particularly if it's something distasteful.

This guy was armed and fired a couple of shots with a semi-automatic pistol, one hitting your hood near the windshield. He was having to stop, so you gunned it by him and turned off onto a farm road to work your way home across the countryside, figuring Rondale Road would be cop-heavy. Most of your adventures had been on Loop 492, but after this one the media started calling you "The Rondale Sniper." Of course, you were not working anything like a sniper, but you guessed it was snappy and fit the headlines.

Getting as hot as the Mideast in August, you decided to lie low for awhile. The cops could only run the Loop and Rondale Road unproductively so many times until they would let their guard down, you thought. You knew that at this point you should stop and relish the memories, retire, so to speak, and be thankful not to have been caught, but you conceded that it had become a need you couldn't control. The days and nights of sitting at home, watching Rondale Road or driving unarmed around town, took on a wistfulness for that high excitement; and yes, you had loved the media. Your purpose had not been to terrorize the public, just the motorists with the bad plates and bad purposes, and you felt the public might understand and maybe empathize if you were arrested and explained.

You waited for a whole month to go out again. There were still a lot of evil drivers who deserved to be terrified, so you loaded your AR-15 a little before five and began cruising the Loop. You passed two city policemen who didn't react to your red pickup, possibly because you had used the black one more, and no cops were in sight when you came up behind a terrible one, an old brown Lincoln with a plate saying "HLL-6066." You did not want to hit the man and didn't. After all, he might have borrowed it. But you pulled onto the shoulder to give yourself a propitious field of fire and riddled the lower trunk. The gasoline tank exploded, and the driver stopped it and got out, running onto the access road, you saw, looking in your rearview mirror. That one alarmed you, so you got off on the nearest exit and headed downtown.

You had always rushed for home before and put your pickup away, but now you had to get off the street any way you could. You stopped outside the Glad to See You Cafe, rolled the windows up, put the rifle on the floorboard under some newspapers and locked the doors. You decided to have something to eat and had just been brought your ribeye steak and baked potato when you noticed the diners leaving. Two men in suits were speaking quietly to them, and they were leaving with their food and drinks on the tables. You had understood that you were caught before the men pulled pistols in front of and behind you and said to put your hands up. You had always intended to submit if confronted and did so.

You have hired an attorney who says he can get you committed to a state hospital. He says you may never be released, but it will still be preferable to prison. You don't disagree. You recognize that your behavior was unacceptable. Your purpose was valid at the outset, but after awhile it became an addiction. "HLL-6066" was an hallucination, you learn.

Texton had a homegrown rock and roll star in the 1950's, Teddy Martin, who called his band "The Songbirds." He was a lovable guy whose big hit was an anthem of teenage love, "Hold Hands." Adding to his mystique, he died in a car wreck at the height of his renown. You have the same name, and your lawyer refers to you by your given name with an intonation aimed at eliciting compassion or pity. He explains the good-bad license plate thing in such a way as to suggest you are bananas. You understand, but you wish he would explain it more comprehensively, which you hope to get a chance to at your committal. Before in Texton, there was one well-known "Teddy." Now there are two, the good one and the bad. You are the bad Teddy.

ANY RUNNING
IS ALL RUNNING

Einstein said you can slow the passage of time by speeding up, and Dante said a slice of time is the same as all time to God. Running is done in space and time, so if what Einstein and Dante said is true, you can freeze time by running fast and any running is all running.

Starting on the quarter-mile graded dirt track during elementary school recess in his school clothes and shoes, the man had always run. For a few years it was in a royal blue, white and silver track uniform and sockless track shoes on springtime Saturdays, running for spectators, a coach and a team. He liked the sensation of speed, the application of strength in the mad yet carefully cultured churning of legs and arms that put wind in his face on a still day and swiftly brought the scenery by on either side.

Running can make you either a hero or a coward, depending on when you run and why. How well you do it does not matter in the cowardly scenario so long as you get away, that is if you value prudence more than gesture. How well you run is important, however, in the heroic milieu. Now that he was into middle age, he ran to keep a semblance of his youthful speed and because he had run once to save a woman›s life and again to preserve his own.

He was in his late twenties in the first instance and had been working out on a hill near his duplex north of a city in Western Colorado, getting pretty fast but not particularly so, he thought. He was having a whiskey and Coke with his wife late one afternoon, looking out the back sliding glass door, when he saw a pickup truck slowly rolling down the long, grassy hill between him and the road he ran on. Barefooted and wearing only slacks, he opened the door, went outside, dropped his drink and scaled the wire fence at the pasture›s edge. He initially thought he could just trot out there and stop it. There was a big brick house at the bottom of the relatively steep hill about fifteen yards past an embankment with a six-foot dropoff. But the heavy old vehicle, which he remembered having seen parked outside a house at the hilltop, suddenly picked up speed and went considerably faster.

He had been loping toward it, moving well but not fast as it was the first time that day he›d run, but now he lowered his head and went flat out, curving slightly to the left to intercept the jouncing, clattering truck. Traversing forty to fifty yards and fortunately not stepping on anything sharp, he caught it some twenty yards before the dropoff. This feat, rare in a life of habitual caution, was made possible by the truck›s having a runningboard onto which he leaped, his hands catching the inside of the open window.

The crucial moment came as he gauged the distance to the house and considered letting it go. Having once been a wheat harvester and knowing about such things, he took a calculated risk that the brake was functional because there was probably somebody home. He fell into the driver›s seat, took the wheel, put his right foot squarely onto the brake pedal, pushed it down and stopped some fifteen feet from the dropoff.

He did not consider leaving it there without notification because he was perturbed that the people at the top of the hill had let it happen. He had always seen the truck parked parallel to the grade on the other side of the road, but it should have had to be sitting nose first to come down the hill. Too wrought up to ring, he went to the front door and knocked. A young woman looked startled by his appearance when she answered, and he looked past her to an ironing board and clothes in the living room by the wall.

"I saw this pickup coming down the hill and ran over and stopped it,» he said, pointing that way with his left arm. "It's right out here!"

A big old man was coming down the grade as the man started home, and he saw the old man and the woman meet and start talking. "Wow, you were really runnin'!'" his wife said. "You really took off!"

The second instance came seven years later. He had been to a record shop across the street from a college in a West Texas city and was trotting across a four-lane intersection with the stoplight when a car came at such high speed that he heard the engine tappets clicking. The driver must have had him fixed at the left-center or center of the hood, and like Lynyrd Skynyrd he needed three steps, moving to the driver›s right, to escape. The car was probably going at least fifty miles an hour, through a red light, because the man was running as fast as he ever had and still sensed or felt the right front bumper almost catch the right heel of his gray patent leather Italian dress shoe. He stopped his trajectory in front of a jewelry store, and the gold watch in a leather pouch that his second wife had just given him went through a previously small hole in his right front pants pocket and landed on the sidewalk.

He ran back to the street to see the car, a gray hotrod with a racing suspension, turn right at the next block and disappear. He wished later that he had gotten the names of some of the witnesses, but he responded like he had in Colorado and went home. He eventually decided that the incident had been about his attempt a few months earlier to collect a debt in a nearby city.

Life is different after the point where you should have violently died. While not the aftermath of an artillery barrage, «brisance» might help the challenging description. The experience became advantageous in a way because there were future tests he was prepared for, having become watchful and harder to surprise. But it was deleterious inasmuch as it colored his enjoyment of living. Insulted and aggrieved, he thought the air smelled differently. It seemed more acrid, somehow, or tainted. It still smelled good at times, but it never smelled the same.

THE LITTLE
RED FOOTSTOOL

Chapter One
"Dr. Gill and Sarah"

The plans and expectations people have upon coming to a small town often turn out to be contrapuntal, especially for educated city people. Each town has its own personality with each one being distinguishable among natives; but they have in common the smaller scale on which everything works. Initially charming, the scale forces new ways of looking and feeling that may grow either to be a comfort or a type of madness.

Dr. Bradley Gill had half-heartedly tried to adjust to his new life in Terkel, Texas, in 1943. He wanted the quick prosperity of a small town practice but was bored with his slender blonde wife, the twenty-bed hospital, the Plains landscape and most sorely his social life. Trim and well-formed at six feet tall with brown hair and eyes, his pretty forehead and cheekbones, dimpled chin and straight nose reminded some people of F. Scott Fitzgerald. He was charismatic on some days and disheveled on others, and patients complained that he seemed distracted.

Like most doctors, he had experimented with drugs. Stimulants in pill form and by injection were used at the parties he had attended at medical school in Galveston and he still often injected himself in the morning to conquer the almost immobilizing narcotic of his ennui. But he was more addicted to the remembered stimuli of his love affair with a little woman with a hard body, dark hair and large, dark eyes. Sarah DesHotel had worked as a nurse in the hospital where he took his residency and he still thought of how she looked at him in the elevator one day, gazing up seriously yet with a mirth that made his palms and belly sweat.

They met at a party organized by older medical students. Sarah had attended regularly and met Brad at the first one he was invited to after transferring from the University of Texas in Austin. They saw each other again the next day and by midnight had a full-fledged love affair going. It was his first really passionate relationship and Sarah was pleased by his fervor. Sometimes he stayed overnight in her second story apartment near the Gulf of Mexico, where they left the windows open to the ocean breeze. Evenings, nights and mornings were not enough, so they met in empty rooms at the hospital.

His ardor began to subside after three months and when he told her in a studied lovers' conversation that he had no immediate plans to marry, she distanced herself in favor of another doctor. He tried to revive the affair and she saw him a few more times; but in the end she said, "I like being with you, Brad, but this guy wants to get married. I got to look out for the future."

He told her again he first wanted to establish a practice, but the truth was that he was uncomfortable with the idea, knowing his family in Fort Worth wouldn't approve. He told himself as he left the apartment that it was just an affair that was over, but he felt more confused and disturbed than he had expected.

She had since been out of his mind for long periods, but in the tedium of life in Terkel she returned with more ferocity than ever. He dwelled on the memories of her low, uncultured voice, the heat of her breath and body, her breathy exclamations and the scents of her hair and perspiration. He thought about her in this mode for almost a year before calling her that summer.

Chapter Two
"Harry's Wedding"

Sarah DesHotel of New Orleans was one of five children in the family of a merchant marine. She became a nurse for the purpose of marrying a doctor and went to Galveston for the medical school and parties. She was there for eight months, having two carefully considered but unproductive affairs, until meeting Dr. Gill.

She began with a rush but realized within a few weeks that he would not work out. She continued for as long as she could, risking trouble with the new resident, because it was her most enjoyable affair, Brad's being quite handsome and newly or freshly awakened. She loved his contoured body and the way he savored her. She would not accept a man who wouldn't give her what she wanted; but she submitted more thoroughly than she ever had, discovering new things about lovemaking and feeling more knowledgeable and fulfilled, to have become truly the woman whom she had often been only trying to portray.

She let him go with some regret but more resolution because Dr. Harry Arnott became obsessive about her even before she took him as a lover. He was a little taller than Brad but pudgy at over two hundred pounds and plain with round wire-rim glasses and a brown felt hat with a short, flat brim. He had more of the proverbial "doctor's look," the slightly off-center, introspective mien suggesting highly developed sensibilities, than did Brad.

Dr. Arnott had done what was necessary, no more, to navigate the curriculum and was ready to take a wife, having denied himself until he was near enough to finishing that he would not be hindered. Not being smooth with women, he had hired prostitutes and inspected them himself to ascertain that they had no diseases, preferring them because he could get better looking ones than the women who were socially available. He had never thought he would become legitimately involved with a woman as pretty and passionate as Sarah. He knew money and social status were his part of the bargain but was happy to make the trade because apart from a culturedness he feigned more than possessed, he was an earthy man who liked coarse women if they were polished enough to put up a social front.

Sarah had hoped for a doctor like Brad but expected one like Harry. She committed to him after the overlap, teaching him to trust her, and they married the next year when his residency was over and he returned to East Texas to practice in Bosque (pronounced Bos-key), near his hometown of Cullum. His father had the best practice in Cullum, a town of thirty-five hundred to Bosque's fifteen hundred, and he planned to move back one day if it looked like he could make more money.

They had a grandiose wedding in the St. Barnabas Methodist Church--the first event Sarah had thoroughly enjoyed since meeting Harry. She was the focus of hushed speculation as gossip circulated, but the prominence and power of the Arnotts was such that it was kept clandestine. Harry was considered to be marrying a trollop of some type and the event had an undercurrent of titillation because he had until then kept his randiness concealed in his hometown.

He sensed what kind of interest there was but didn't care. He considered himself superior to the townspeople and knew Sarah's pedigree would be less important in Bosque and obscure in ten or fifteen years. His relatives kept any dismay to themselves and greeted the couple with complete approval, partly because of the weight he carried as a new physician but also because there was a side of him that made disapproval of his choice unwise. He was normally cheerful and affected an easy-goingness, but he was a hater who, once alienated, could be intractable.

Harry LePoiner Arnott developed an emphatic and sometimes bitterly expressed enmity for the Japanese and Germans, but it was in a way disingenuous. His real hatred was for injuries to his pride. Unbeknownst to all but a few citizens of the state, he was, if sufficiently provoked, one of the most dangerous otherwise sane and productive members of the social upper class in Texas.

He had two sisters and was the only medical person in the family other than his father and grandfather. His dad, Dr. Anthony Arnott, had indulged him greatly because he showed an early interest and apparent aptitude that was for the most part faked. His mother, the half-French, red-haired Genevieve LePoiner of Houston, was often distressed by his behavior but left him more in his father's charge. Harry knew he had abnormal emotions at times, but he never got into trouble and did not think of himself as a potential criminal. Indeed, with a modicum of luck, he might have gotten through life with his failings and vulnerabilities being no more than a family secret, as many men do.

Chapter Three
"New Orleans Romance"

"Sarah?"

"Yes?"

"It's Brad."

"Uh. . ."

"How're you doing?"

"Okay. How're you?"

Pretty good. I keep thinking about you."

"Where are you?"

"A little town in the Panhandle, Terkel."

Brad's call was welcome. Harry had been proffering a kind of conviviality that she tried to reciprocate, but his intensity and the dull small town had made her restless. She had often reminisced about Brad in the long, silent days in the big brick house and now her pulse surged in her head and made her slightly dizzy.

"I should have married you, Sarah."

"Nothin' we can do about it now."

"I can't forget you. I think about us all the time."

"Brad." She looked around, but of course Harry was at the office. She started to tell Brad she could not resume their affair, but she suddenly wanted to. Her body warmed and became more fluid and graceful as she stood there breathing slowly into the phone.

"Sarah?"

"Call me tomorrow. I need time to think."

"I'm not asking you to give up anything. I'd just like to see you again. . . a few times."

"Call me back."

She asked the next day if he could meet her in New Orleans the next month when she visited her family. He said he'd contrive to. "Who did you marry, Brad?"

"A girl from Fort Worth. I'm fond of her, but we don't fit like I thought we would."

"You remember Harry."

"Sure." Remembering Harry was part of what gave Brad the confidence to call her. He had been cordial to them after the breakup but stayed away from her, not wanting to be rebuffed again. But he felt much superior to the other man and hoped the difference was by now reason for Sarah's wry regret. "How's he doing?"

"Okay. People been goin' to Cullum to see his daddy, so they took right to him."

She had originally thought Brad was unwilling to marry her because of her unculturedness and he would choose another woman in deference to his family of doctors and other rich people. She still felt as though she were somewhere below him looking up but now took heart in knowing she had a stronger hold on him, in an important way, than his wife.

Brad made the excuse of going to New Orleans to look for medical equipment and Sarah arranged to go for a couple of days during the week so Harry could not accompany her. Marty had left the previous weekend to see her family and Harry resolved to visit New Orleans with Sarah in the future.

Sarah saw her mother for a few hours to cover her trail in case Harry called but spent the rest of her time with Brad at the rococo Saints Arms Hotel. It was the most concentrated debauchery either of them had ever undertaken. Brad brought stimulants with which they injected themselves periodically, balancing that with room service wine and whiskey. They went out to eat but were staring into each other's eyes before the dinner was brought and cut short the outing to return to the room.

They broke away once a day to call their spouses and lie enthusiastically. Marty was nice to Brad, but Sarah thought there was a trace of malice in Harry's voice. She went back to Brad smoothly enough but resolved to be careful when she went home.

It was the kind of extended other-worldly experience they had both long wanted. As much danger as there was in it, their time let them discover the "two become as one" phenomenon. In their debauchery as it should have been in their marriage, the difference between male and female was negligible. They were not themselves or each other anymore; they were one thing, more than double what they had been apart and less overwhelmed by the drugs, alcohol and carnality than by the revelation of one of the essential secrets of the universe, the power and beauty there is in the resolution of "a two."

Even if Brad never wanted to marry her, Sarah was still glad she had done it. Paying critical attention to his eyes when he said he loved her, she thought maybe she was fooling herself, but it really seemed like he meant it. He was so enraptured that she could not imagine his ever letting her go again. They lay still for awhile before hunger overwhelmed them and they leaped up, laughing as they dressed, to rush to a streetside restaurant and eat seafood and drink chablis. They strolled through Andrew Jackson Park just after dark, stopped, embraced under the radiant moon and kissed. "I love you, Brad," she said.

"I love you, too. This is romantic."

He felt a strong attachment but had no intention of leaving Marty because his family would have disapproved and he planned eventually to go back to Fort Worth. What he loved was the eroticism. He took a genteel approach to sensual matters and treated Sarah politely, almost like a formal acquaintance, except in their intimate sphere.

He wanted one more time with her, but his flight was leaving for Dallas and he had to go right after they returned to the Saints Arms three blocks off Bourbon Street. She waved goodbye as he gave her a thumbs-up through the taxi's rear window. She came down five minutes later to hail a ride to her mother's big apartment near the Mississippi River. Brad was going to lay over in Dallas to rest and collect himself and she needed to do the same.

Chapter Four
"Home with Harry"

Sarah concocted a series of strategems and counter-strategems to use with Harry or that he might try on her. They seemed endless the more she thought about it, but she was just trying to be prudent and was not really apprehensive because she was prepared to leave if he ever threatened or hurt her. His idiosyncracies would have been less vexatious if he had not been so disturbed. She wouldn't have been so susceptible to Brad if Harry had been more normal, she thought.

"Hi, honey!" she called to him behind the rope on the runway. He waved back, smiling artificially. He took her suitcase and hugged her sideways in a tentative, exploratory way that made her skin crawl. "I hope you didn't mind me takin' a couple o' extra days," she said. "It'd been a long time since I seen 'em."

"I didn't. Been looking forward to getting you back."

He goosed her under the arm by her breast, but she had braced herself and did not flinch. She fell asleep when they got home and he left for the office and she did not awaken until he gingerly woke her, naked and cuddling. "Are you glad to see me?" she asked.

"You bet! I'm always glad to see you." He did not know what was wrong with her trip but was suspicious. She had sounded nervous on the phone and stayed too long. But he did not want to believe she was two-timing him on so little evidence and would wait to be sure.

Chapter Five
"Unfinished Business"

Brad and Sarah rendezvoused twice more during the next year. They waited six months between times and resolved to make the third time their last for a longer period. Sarah started staying more at her mother's and going to the hotel to see Brad, who even returned with some medical equipment to validate his story. Sarah took Harry with her between assignations to see her relatives.

Harry thought he knew what she was doing after the second trip and was certain before she was back from the third. Mulling his suspicions, he tried to think of whom she could be seeing. He had made her tell him her sexual history after they married. She had deleted parts of it, of course, but told him about Brad because she thought he might already know.

Harry called Brad's office in Terkel when Sarah left for the second time and was told Dr. Gill was in New Orleans on business. He thought it could be a coincidence, but after her third departure and another report that Dr. Gill was in New Orleans, he was sure.

What affected him worst was the realization that both Gill and Sarah must see him as the less exciting, less attractive man.

The thought of their derision made him feel hotter and meaner than he had ever felt. He considered going there and killing them but played the scene through in his mind and realized he did not want to kill Sarah, just Gill. His writhing brain told him he could only get even with Gill by killing him. The imperative to kill Dr. Gill had him grunting and making rhythmical movements like an animal in his big leather chair in the den.

Harry was pleasant and made light conversation upon her return, soft-shouldering the dark blue Buick out of Dallas and over the forest-sided roads of East Texas to Bosque. He waited until they were sitting in the den with drinks to say, "I know you've been seeing Dr. Gill, but I still want us to stay together."

Sarah had been preparing for this and was not going to lie first and tearfully repent. "Don't think I don't regret it because I do. I won't see him anymore if that helps. It's over." Brad had finally told her he could not marry her. In their last hours together they stupefied themselves with liquor, two final injections and lovemaking in which Sarah turned her head. "I don't know what to say," she said, puffing a cigarette and sipping her drink. "I'm sorry?"

"You don't have to say anything. Sometimes old flames take awhile to die out."

"That's all it was, unfinished business. I'd like to forget it if I can."

"It's already forgotten as far as I'm concerned if he'll do one thing--apologize."

"You mean go see him?"

"I could get over it better. I won't get mad."

She had never been able to read him very well and was afraid he was being false. She couldn't tell anything as he sat there placidly with one hand under his chin, bobbing his head as he talked. "I'd rather not," she said.

"I know, but you won't have to do anything but call him. It would help me," he said, patting her knee.

Eerie as it was, his being too nice was hard for her to be skeptical about because she hadn't expected him to be conciliatory or even rational. She thought he might be playing some sinister game that she had to play along with without knowing what it was.

Chapter Six
"Something Maddening"

Marty Gill had long felt something maddening was forcing its way into her life. She was trying to disguise the intermittent depression she felt but thought it must be related to the war with the Germans being on the verge of defeat. Drs. Arnott and Gill had been exempted from service because they practiced in rural areas where there was a dearth of doctors. The phone started ringing at ten o'clock that night.

"Hello," said Marty.

"Is Dr. Gill there?" Sarah asked.

"Yes. Honey!"

"Ask who it is."

"Whom shall I say is calling?"

"Mrs. Arnott, Sarah."

Brad had expected no more than some type of embarrassment if Harry learned of the affair, but he still did not want to take the phone to talk to Sarah in front of his wife. "They're old med school friends," he said, getting up. "I wonder what they're up to now. Hello," he said brightly.

"Brad, he knows."

"Where are you?"

"Phone booth outside town."

"Oh? What have you been up to?"

"He made me come up here. He wants to talk."

"Right! I'd invite you to stay, but we don't have the room."

"Who is it, Brad?" Marty asked.

"Just a minute," he told Sarah before shielding the phone and telling Marty, "They're passing through on vacation. They're staying at a motel here, old party friends," he said, rolling his eyes. "Hello, Sarah?"

"He's settin' there watchin' me. I don't think he's goin' back unless you talk to him."

"I'm sorry, Sarah. I'm bushed. Why don't I come by in the morning?"

"He's just gonna keep makin' me call. I don't think he'll do anything but talk."

"I'm sorry, I can't make it tonight. Tell Harry next time. Good night." He hung up.

"Harry Arnott," he said to Marty. "He's tying one on and wants me to drink with him."

"Is he a doctor?"

"Yeah, in East Texas. They're on the way to New Mexico."

"Go over and see him if you want to."

"I really don't. I'm tired. I don't want anything to drink."

Harry made Sarah call every fifteen minutes for an hour and a half and Marty had to keep answering in case it was the hospital. Sarah made each call more insistent than the last, finally making a reference to Brad's med school reputation as a voluptuary to shorten the ordeal. Marty grew more and more distressed and prevailed on Brad to talk to Sarah again at half-past eleven after going to bed herself and getting up twice.

"Sarah, I don't feel like going out."

"Please, Brad."

"Why are you doing this?"

"I agreed with him, he deserves an apology. I thought you'd come."

"All right!" he said, muffling his mouth with his hand. "But I don't ever wanta see or hear of either one o' you again!"

"Couple o' miles out o' town, Texton highway."

He hung up, really perturbed and thinking he might just break old homely Harry's nose. He can learn not to mess with me! he thought.

Chapter Seven
"Don't Tell Anybody"

Just after midnight on that starry April night, Brad parked his gray Packard coupe behind the Arnotts and he and Harry got out into the sweet night air. There was no question of Brad's punching Harry, though, because Harry unhesitatingly brought up a pistol and fired, shouting, "Don't you know this is my wife?" The first bullet missed the left side of Brad's head by fewer than six inches and the second almost hit him squarely in the belly button, going in an inch low and to the right.

Being a young man in good condition, he saved his life by not falling but running to his right away from the cars and into the darkness of the cotton field. With Sarah screaming and Harry cursing, the Buick whirled and shone its headlights into the field. Harry swept the field, urgently seeking Dr. Gill because he did not intend to leave him alive; but a car was coming down the two-lane asphalt highway and he left the scene.

With her terror when Harry started hunting Brad after pulling the big long-barrel police model .38-caliber revolver from under the seat and shooting him, Sarah was for the first time in her life so scared that she could not move or say anything. She was afraid Harry would kill her, too. She had seen Brad hit and thought he was dying. She didn't realize Harry had made her an accomplice. She had seen Brad grimace, fall halfway to the ground and, face agonized and pathetic, stagger away. Harry was holding the pistol in his lap with one hand and steering with the other as she gauged the distance in sidelong glances, gathering her nerve to try to grab it, when he said mellifluously, "I'm sorry, Sarah."

He turned and gave her what he meant to be a look of perfect compassion. "I didn't want to deceive you, but I just had to get him and I knew you wouldn't go along. I hope you know I wouldn't hurt you. Can I put the gun up? I'm going to throw it away as soon as we get to a lake."

"Hell bell's, Harry, don't you know we're in trouble?"

"Maybe; we'll get out of it."

"I never thought you'd do somethin' like that."

"I've got plenty o' money, lot o' friends. I might do some time, but not much."

"What about me?"

"You won't do any time, Sarah."

She sat stiffly as he turned on the radio, tuning in a favorite big band station, and stayed that way while he stopped at a lake near Ploughman to throw the gun in. They ate in an all-night restaurant in Early and were home, with his pushing the Buick haphazardly to eighty miles an hour as the night shortened, by daybreak.

Brad had run as far as he could and watched Dr. Arnott's car, wriggling into the soil and pressing his right cheek down with his palms flat on each side of his head until the Buick left.

He crawled out of the field on all fours, holding his abdomen and crying, and lay on the roadside until another car came and he hailed it, pushed up sideways on his right shoulder and feebly waving both arms and hands in front of and slightly above him. "I'm a doctor," he said. "Some people robbed me."

"What do you want me to do?" asked the motorist, a slick-haired salesman in a wide-lapel suit.

"Take me to the hospital. Don't tell anybody."

Chapter Eight
"Official Bi'ness"

He did not want to give the factual account of what had happened, of course. But after surgery and two days at Birdsong Memorial Hospital in Texton during which the attack was reported and became the subject of gossip over much of West Texas and parts of New Mexico and Oklahoma, Brad saw he couldn't stay with the story he told at the hospital, that he had been out driving and stopped to help two men who shot him and fled without robbing him. Victory County Sheriff Tag Tankersley knew that was not the real story and on the afternoon of the second day cajoled him into telling the truth.

"If you know who shot you, you better tell me so we can pick him up. Besides that, you don't want to perjure yourself."

With great alarm, Brad thought he could have made up a better story if he hadn't been so shocked and in so much pain. He felt absurd protecting Dr. Arnott. Who would have thought he was such a maniac? Along with recognizing the untenability of his account, he knew what the other man was now and was afraid he would try again. He told the sheriff who the assailant was but maintained he did not know why Dr. Arnott had shot him. He was in such emotional and physical anguish that he was blubbering in spasms of remorseful sobbing.

Hanging his head, Tankersley left to issue a warrant for Dr. Arnott. Marty met him in the hall and asked, "What did he say?"

"He'll have to tell you. Give 'im awhile an' go in."

"It was Dr. Arnott, wasn't it?"

"You can get it from your husban', Miz Gill. Excuse me now. I got to go do some official bi'ness."

She had immediately known what happened. She remembered the strained, peculiar conversations with Sarah, whom she knew only as a vulgarian and an emotional rapist, with disgust. Marty hated the scandal she knew was everywhere but regretted the personal aspects of it more. She was not surprised that Brad had had an affair. She was just sickened by its extraordinary salacity and dismayed that he had so publicly besmirched himself and come so close to being murdered. She had no familiarity with any of this and was bereft of her natural bearings as she went down the hall and into the room. "Did you talk to the sheriff?" Brad asked.

"Yeah."

"Did he tell you?"

"I guess. . . I know."

"I'm sorry, Marty," said Brad, bowing his head and trying to regurgitate some of the remorse he had shown to Tankersley. "I must have been crazy, but good God!" He sobbed and looked at her with tears refilling his eyes.

He was in periodically excruciating pain and it grabbed him now, making him howl in earnest and prompting her to embrace him, crying and stroking his hair. She was normally a pleasant, hopeful-looking woman with well-shaped cheekbones, blonde hair cut short and big, wide open green eyes. But it was not the natural woman who was talking to Dr. Gill as the warrant was going out for Dr. Arnott but the haunted, fragile one she had been evolving into that day.

"She said he just wanted to talk," Brad said. "That's all we thought he was doing. The affair was over. I won't ever do it again. You won't divorce me, will you?"

"Now is not the right time to ask."

Chapter Nine
"The Couples"

Marty bore most of the scrutiny because Dr. Gill stayed indoors most of the time for two months. She hated her trips out because of people's expressions when they stared or stole glances. They looked so repulsive. She was discomfited but not embarrassed because she hadn't done anything wrong. Brad's parents evinced unflagging support, waiting for the uproar to die down and hoping it would one day be forgotten.

Being in a town like Terkel was in a way helpful because its few doctors were looked on as almost godlike by much of the citizenry and as too indispensable to be dealt with on an ordinary plane by the rest. Dr. Gill had patients not just in Terkel but from miles around and while he wasn't as beloved as some had been, he was a competent physician and a usually congenial man who still held the sensitive place in people's lives that doctors do. He found all he had to do was play "doctor," be serious and businesslike, and he had no more than a few annoying remarks or questions, quickly or softly spoken, that he could easily ignore.

Sarah was charged with attempted murder a few days after her husband was arrested and released on bond. It was an event from which Marty, remembering Sarah's remark that she knew how much Brad liked parties because she "used to be his girlfriend," derived much secret satisfaction. Harry was going to be tried first and the district attorney told Brad he thought it would be a year. The Gills' life calmed as the weeks passed and at times seemed almost irenic. Brad was very solicitous, fearing Marty would divorce him. Their little girl Katy was fortunately not school age, so they refined an insular, if somewhat brittle, new life.

Harry and Sarah passed their time similarly, but Harry was cheerier than Brad and Sarah glummer than Marty. Their tack was that they were in Bosque all the time and did not know why the Gills were making such accusations. Dr. Arnott told it around town that Dr. Gill was a drug addict and must have been shot by some underworld character. He said Dr. Gill and he had been rivals for Sarah and he won, fomenting Dr. Gill's enmity. By saying Dr. Arnott had shot him, Dr. Gill could cover the seedy truth. The Bosqueites of course took the Arnotts' side and their support made it easier for Sarah. What bothered her was that she saw the same looks on people's faces that Marty did. It was a situation people in neither place knew how to deal with. It was disturbing but fascinating because the people understood, regardless what they said to the principals, what had happened.

The Gills were nominal Methodists who only went on Easter and Christmas, but the Arnotts were First Christian Church members who attended weekly. They found religion useful to mollify their image and listened in an ostensibly attentive way but with total self-absorption one Sunday morning as the bushy white-haired Dr. Marshall Menzies preached on the availability of inner peace.

Invoking Philippians 4:8-9, he said, "Finally, brethren, whatsoever things are true, whatsoever things are honorable, whatsoever things are just, whatsoever things are pure, whatsoever things are lovely, whatsoever things are of good report, if there be any virtue and if there be any praise, think on these things. The things which ye both learned and received and heard and saw in me, these things do and the God of peace shall be with you."

Chapter Ten
"He Don't Squeal"

The fifteen months between the shooting and trial were a kind of solstice. The Gills turned to each other with a desperation that made them closer and more comforting to each other than ever while the Arnotts indulged in experiments that, not surprisingly, Harry found more enjoyable than Sarah. Brad was anxious to prove himself and please Marty at levels he had never taken the trouble to reach. She responded and her spring-wound cleaving engendered a new tenderness in him. They dreaded the trial but looked forward to its aftermath as a time when the ordeal would be over.

In their concentration on each other as a form of security, Brad introduced Marty to the things he most enjoyed. They left Katy in Fort Worth and vacationed in Santa Fe. She did not need liquor or drugs, but he persuaded her to let him inject her in the motel room as they drank and laughed through the hazy interludes. She understood better now what made him happy and would do anything to put more certainty into their lives, although she found drugs and alcohol a hindrance.

Harry knew Sarah would not leave him now so long as he didn't get too rough. She had been charged, too, and needed him to pay her legal expenses. With his new confidence, he coaxed her into letting him tie her up and put her in hiding places around the house. Giggling and baby talking, he would look for her as though he did not know where she was, covered with a black cloth. He liked to tie her on the bed and once made her threaten to leave by getting out a new .38 he had bought. For a long time, Sarah did not understand her life anymore. But with her cooperation, Harry started to behave normally more of the time. It was a strange rapport from which they took a perverse comfort. Really hurting her would not have fit into Harry's mode of reason, but not letting Dr. Gill win out, no matter what the cost, made sense. If he were convicted and imprisoned, that would again put Gill one up in their humiliation contest.

No one in town questioned his defense, but the real core of sympathy was not based on their acceptance of his account. It was on the perception of him as a justifiably enraged cuckold. Many felt that, doctor or not, he had responded in the proper masculine manner. Some told him they remembered seeing him in town that day. Others said to his discouragement that they had seen his car parked outside his home all afternoon and night and volunteered to testify that he could not have been four hundred miles away in the Panhandle. His story was that Sarah and he had taken a ninety-minute drive that late afternoon and early evening and his attorneys did not want to put any obvious liars on the stand.

Harry took a call one day at work from someone whose voice sounded familiar but who requested anonymity. It sounded like a man named Ritter whose family he treated and who had just gotten out of the penitentiary after serving two years for stealing lumber in a neighboring county. "There's a guy in Dallas could help you," the voice said. "A pro, real coldblooded."

"Oh? What's his name?"

"Tex Wilkie. You can get ahold of him through his brother, got a garage."

"A professional, you say?"

"Yeah."

"Well, I don't know what I'd need him for, but I appreciate it."

"I know him. He don't squeal."

"Oh, he doesn't?"

"Naw."

Harry thanked the man and hung up. He was near the end of the day and had sent his nurse home. He leaned back with a daydreaming look and thought of his trial, a month away. He had been less hopeful because the Gills were going ahead with their testimony. He would have let it drop if he had been exonerated, but he thought, Gill is healthy and happy again, probably doesn't even know the difference. His people'll back him like mine do me and they'll convict me. The trial would in Terkel.

Harry thought Gill would not be alive and about to send him to prison if he had used a professional killer. The conversation he had just had was convincing and he found himself, as when he had raised the pistol to shoot Gill, mechanically and somewhat surrealistically picking up the phone, getting information and writing the number of Wilkie's Garage in Dallas.

He felt it would be naive to think he could start arranging it that easily, but he was sure that if what he had been told was true, Tex Wilkie's brother would not betray him. The brother must provide protection, he thought. He was confident the call had been from an ex-convict who told the truth as he knew it because there was real advocacy in his voice. He had thought of asking him to make the contact, but that would have been too risky. He wanted to make the call but was afraid it would be too unconventional in the criminal world and be discounted. He sat back and thought of everything that had happened, sharpening his fighting mood and trying to clear his mind and make it agile. Then he relaxed and smiled, thinking, I'll ask my lawyer about this man. That's the kind of thing lawyers are good for.

Chapter Eleven
"Tex"

Tex Wilkie was proof in the living flesh that rather than being anything, evil is more essentially the absence of things. His was a real killer's look, not the demented one that sometimes came over Dr. Arnott but the insouciant, mildly chuckling one that says, I know secrets few people know and what you think is awesome is really more like a joke.

He was five feet, nine inches tall with sandy blond hair, dark blue eyes, long, full features and tight, waxy skin. He had weighed one hundred eighty-five pounds when he shot it out in 1943 with a Blackland County deputy on the Texas High Plains, trying to kill a man scheduled to testify against him in a burglary case; one sixty-five after jumping furlough and one-fifty or less at times when in jail. More average-looking in his healthier forms, the skinnier he got, the more reptilian he looked. His eyes became more prominent with hard, dark pupils and flat lids across the tops so he looked like what he was, a human snake.

The people most afraid of him were those who knew him best: criminal associates, relatives, girlfriends, ex-girlfriends and lawyers. One who had represented him often was Ronald "Jelly" Barnes, who regarded him as "a man who has no feelings."

After breaking into the underworld as a gunman in the Texas and Louisiana bootlegger wars of the 1920s, Wilkie prospered as a burglar and killer, specializing in dynamite-rigging cars. He only had convictions for assault, attempted murder and burglary, but the Texas Rangers estimated he had killed more than twenty people, mostly other hoodlums.

He had attended Texas Baptist College in his hometown of Corsairs in Southeast Texas for two years with the ambition of becoming a physician. He worked in various jobs at the medical school and during three years in prison was a valued nurse and operating room assistant, learning the use of chloroform for the later purpose of knocking out burglary victims.

Wilkie was drafted out of college in 1917 but did not go overseas to fight. He never returned to school but took to the criminal lifestyle and at forty-six had had no more than minor convictions and incarcerations. He was one the most feared criminals in the state in knowledgeable circles but had been so polished that he never got much publicity and was not seriously sought after when he failed to appear at the end of his sixty-day furlough for treatment of a leg wound inflicted by the deputy. He was in Dallas with a barmaid who was not known as one of his women. He'd been hoping for work when, two weeks before Dr. Arnott's trial, he learned Harry wanted to meet him.

Harry had hired a lawyer in his East Texas hometown of Bosque and top Dallas criminal attorney Hal Harrison after shooting Dr. Gill. He called Harrison ostensibly to talk about his case and asked about Wilkie, saying a friend had told him the man would be a likely choice if Dr. Gill hired someone to kill him. The lawyer confirmed the gravity of anything pertinent to Wilkie and gave Harry a sketch of what he knew.

Harry took his Sarah with him to meet Harrison and called Wilkie's brother Jack from the hotel. He surmised he would be taken more seriously if he related his legal trouble, so he told Jack Wilkie he would go on trial for attempted murder in two weeks and would pay well "for a job." He left his number and Tex called that night.

"Dr. Arnott," he said pleasantly.

"This is Tex," Wilkie said in his softly modulated voice.

"Uh, yes," Harry said, smiling at Sarah. "I was wondering if we could talk."

Wilkie told him to park fifteen yards past the gate at the Pearly Gates Cemetery at ten o'clock. He arrived thirty minutes early, stopped nearby and hid behind a monument. He had called a lawyer he knew in Texton after setting the meeting and learned there was such a case about to be tried. He was sure it was legitimate, so to speak, but wanted to look Dr. Arnott over first.

Harry arrived, emerged and lit a cigarette, illuminating his face. It would be risky, but Tex wanted a big pay day so he would not have to work for awhile. He did not smoke, drink heavily or gamble except for small stakes. He'd never been prone to waste money because it was one of the things he liked best along with expensive clothes, good cars and easy-going, closed-mouth women. He perused the richly attired physician and his heavy new car and knew this would be his biggest score ever. He moved through foliage and approached Harry from around a corner in the road with a composed expression but with eagerness in his heart like a teenage job applicant.

"Doctor," he said with a deliberate lilt, not offering his hand out of deference.

"Yes!" Harry held out his hand and warmly shook Tex's. "Shall we get in the car?"

They settled into the Buick and sat silently with Tex looking out the front and Harry glancing at him. "Should I tell you about the job?"

"Uh-huh."

"It's Dr. Bradley Gill in Terkel, Texas. I shot him and he's fixing to testify on me."

"Has he got a family?"

"Wife and a kid."

"How old is the kid?"

"Little, shouldn't be a problem."

"The woman?"

Harry paused. "Do you think it'll be necessary?"

"Could be."

"Do it if you have to."

"Do you know where he lives?" Wilkie asked.

"Never been there."

"I'll find it."

"The fee?"

"Fifteen thousand in advance."

The amount surprised Harry. He had brought part of it and would have to borrow the remainder, having depleted his bank account for legal fees. But he didn't argue because Tex never identified a client, no matter what the pressure.

"A doctor is bound to bring heat. I may need a lawyer. Once I'm paid, I never contact you again."

"Well, I guess you get what you pay for," said Harry, pulling an envelope from his coat. "I've got five thousand on me. Can I meet you back here with the rest?"

"Any time," said Tex, taking it with a light heart and agreeing to meet in the cemetery in exactly a week. "Any preference on the time?"

"After the trial in two weeks. It'd be too obvious if we did it before."

"How long after?"

"Any time. The sooner, the better."

Chapter Twelve
"The Night of His Return"

Harry still might have called it off if he had been acquitted because he knew Gill's murder would cause a furor and he would be widely blamed. He had little hope, though, and thought it best to deal decisively with Wilkie while he had the chance. His blood lust was up and while he would have written off the money with an acquittal, he was better prepared to see it through to the logical conclusion. At the end of his reasoning, he still felt the other man deserved to die. He met Wilkie in the cemetery again and gave him the money in one hundred dollar bills in a spare doctor's bag. "When do you think it'll happen?" he asked.

"Two or three weeks after the trial. I don't like to work too fast, but I'll do it as soon as I'm ready."

"Well," said Harry, offering Wilkie his hand. "Good luck."

Tex disappeared into the cemetery and Harry backed out and started home. Feeling more placid than he had in a long time, he clicked on the radio and hummed to Whispering Jack Smith's "Crazy Rhythm" as he drove south out of town. Tex had wanted his money in advance so he would have no trouble collecting it and to leave it with someone he trusted until the heat was off. He certainly didn't want to be caught with it and lose it.

Conducted in the week of the Tehran Conference and thus upstaged by Stalin, Churchill and Roosevelt, the trial went as Harry expected. Brad said Dr. Arnott had shot him but maintained he didn't know why, although he testified Harry had shouted, "Don't you know this is my wife?" and left no doubt of the motive.

A half-dozen Bosqueites swore Harry was in town at times when it would have been impossible for him later to have driven to Terkel. Dr. Gill's wife Marty said a woman identifying herself as Mrs. Arnott called numerous times that night and forced Dr. Gill to meet her on the Texton Highway. Neither Harry nor Sarah took the stand.

The jury deliberated for two hours and came back with a five-year term. Harry took care not to look vindictive, standing around the courtroom and in the hall outside and commenting for all to hear, "Well, I'm not too surprised. I figured we'd lose up here in Dr. Gill's home territory. We'll reverse it on appeal."

The Gills were in extreme discomfiture throughout the trial and left immediately. "I guess we're lucky he got anything," said Brad in the car.

"Do you think she'll get anything?" Marty asked.

"The DA doubts it."

Tex drove to Terkel from Dallas five days later and never got out of the car except to check a telephone directory at a service station for the address. He drove at twilight to look at the Gills' beige-blond brick house on the city's nicest street, six blocks west of downtown, and the dark neighborhood. He stayed just long enough to get the layout and visualize his movements for the night of his return.

Chapter Thirteen
"The Little Red Footstool"

To Thomas "Tex" Wilkie, it was just another criminal adventure, albeit the biggest of his life. He took a few days to spend some of the money and stayed in Blackland a hundred miles away. He put up in a cheap hotel and contacted a garageman whom he had known for a long time, Blackie McNeese. McNeese well knew what Wilkie was but knew he was a professional who would protect him. McNeese had a teenage son from whom Wilkie bought a pair of black tennis shoes and he came back at night when no one was in the garage to buff the tread off. Tex had a former girlfriend who was living with an ex-convict he knew and he arranged to rent one of their cars, a 1940 black Ford, for Thursday night. The couple knew Tex was using them to advance a criminal enterprise, but it had been a long time since anyone who knew him had told him "no" about anything. Knowing his reputation better than anyone, he used his easy charm to smooth his operations, approaching politely, smiling often and making quiet, wry jokes to soften the effect.

He had supper at a cafe near his hotel and lingered over coffee and the newspaper, the Blackland Pictorial. He went for the car at eight, parking the tan 1939 Dodge he had borrowed from his brother, and drove south at a leisurely pace. He had called a woman in Houston the day before and said he would see her in two days. He chose her because he had used her in a killing four years earlier and was certain, based on her dummied-up response to officers then, that she would tell investigators nothing. He got into Terkel at ten-thirty and drove southeast toward Texton to kill another thirty minutes. He timed fifteen minutes and headed back, enjoying the car's peppiness.

The alley behind the house was as dark and quiet as usual when he wheeled slowly into it from the east. He shut off the ignition and coasted to a stop, opening his door. He sat there to see if anyone would investigate, but no one showed. He had stopped between the Gill house and the one next door so the people in each might assume he was visiting the other. He had taped the interior light switches flat inside the doors and there was no light when he got out wearing the tennis shoes and carrying Dr. Arnott's bag with his burglary tools.

Tex circled the house again and again, peeking into windows until he was sure everyone was asleep and the child would not wake up. He found an unlocked window and stretched to push it up far enough to get his head and shoulders through. There was nothing outside to boost himself off and he had to jump, catch himself on his arms and look in through the curtains. In his most athletically demanding feat of the night, he came down on the windowsill on his belly and grunted to himself, straining fiercely to maintain silence. Right under the window was a red footstool with a scowling blue cat's face across the top. He looked around the room, saw the five-year-old girl sleeping in her bed and then saw the footstool. It was a foot high, so he got it and dropped back to the ground.

He put on rubber gloves, not surgical gloves but thicker laboratory worker's gloves, flesh-colored and snug. He wanted to move with dispatch now that everything was in order. He set the footstool and stepped on it, jumped, put the bag in and wriggled slowly through the window and onto the floor. He lay there for a minute, listening, and only heard Katy's breathing. He sat up meticulously and then got up and moved into the hallway. He opened the bag and put on his mask, which covered his whole head with slits for the eyes and mouth. He took out his heavy short barrel .44-caliber revolver, closed the bag and carried the pistol in his right hand and the bag in his left.

He passed a bathroom on the left and knew the open door at the hall's end was the doctor's bedroom. His eyes adjusted to the gloom with the pupils crowding out the irises. He made out Brad's face on the other side of the bed and moved deliberately around; but coming within six feet, he stepped quickly, pressed the muzzle between the beatifically sleeping eyes and pulled the trigger. Marty awoke in a state of perfect emotional suspension, started to rise and was hit hard in the head. She could not rise again but, though essentially unconscious, was terrified at the most basic level and started moaning and making agonized movements as if having a nightmare.

Tex put down the bag, took out a roll of packing twine and began wrapping Marty to Brad. He wrapped and wrapped until he did not think she could get loose. He didn't finish her because he was wearing the mask and she could not identify him. It was just a commercial job and he would not do any more than the contract called for. Marty kept moaning and moving slightly, tied tightly Brad back to back. Tex had stepped into the shadows by the dresser when he heard the little girl.

Katy had awakened when the gun went off. It was plenty loud enough to wake her, even muffled by her father's head. She toddled in in her white nightgown, sucking her thumb, and the man in the mask grabbed her. He opened his chloroform bottle and carried her into the hall, opened the closet, pushed her in and splashed the liquid on her. "Don't, don't!" she cried, fighting with her arms. He piled clothes, laid her on them, closed the door and returned to the bedroom.

Marty was quieting down and becoming part of the gruesome bundle. Tex watched for awhile and realized with the little letting-go he sometimes felt that she would die, too. He put everything into the bag, went into Katy's room and closed the window. He peered outside and went out the back door. Looking all around, he ran in a dog trot to the car, turned on the lights when he was out of the alley and met one slow-moving farm pickup on his way north out of town.

Katy woke up at seven a.m., opened the closet and went in to see her parents. At first she could not understand. Then her eyes got bigger, popping out more, her mouth opened wide and she just stood there looking. The incredible look in her eyes was still there years later. The conventional description would be that it was horrified, but it was more than that. If you had looked right into her eyes, you would have seen that something had been murdered in there. Wilkie had been merciful in his way, but the worst murder took place in those flashing instants as the innocence in Katy Gill's beautiful blue eyes throbbed, shrank and died.

She thought of going to a neighbor lady's, reared back, slowly whirled to the open door and walked stiffly through the hall to the kitchen door. Mrs. Chumley was outside getting her newspaper and saw the child coming across the lawn. "Katy, is something wrong?" she called. Seeing her expression, the woman asked, "What in the world?" Something caught her eye above and to the right of the little girl's head. It was where Tex had left it, standing with its red oak legs pressed into the dirt: the little red footstool.

Chapter Fourteen
"Big Daddy"

Tex gunned the Ford to eighty and better most of the way to Blackland and switched cars. The Dodge was a souped-up number he knew would run relentlessly and he drove it hard through the night to reach Houston by noon Friday. He stopped on a bridge at Tonkawa Creek Reservoir south of Corsairs and dropped in the bag with the burglary tools, gun and tennis shoes, cutting it with his knife to make it sink. He had told the woman, a skinny but buxom dark-haired creature named Ronni Dale, that he might need her for an alibi. "Sure, Tex," she had said. "You know you can count on me."

Sheriff Tag Tankersley was unready for the Gills' bedroom and left when he felt the nausea. The child was taken by Dr. Gill's parents and Tag shut the house after the bodies were removed. He had interviewed Katy, recognized chloroform was used and called the Texas Rangers. He checked the alley and made casts of partial tire prints, but the alley was hard and the prints were indistinctive.

Ned Tomes was in his middle fifties and known, among other things, for having been among the half-dozen lawmen who ambushed Bonnie and Clyde in Louisiana in 1934. At five foot-ten and mostly bald with a small pot belly, he still played the part of a Ranger with elan. With the rest of the Bonnie and Clyde party, he had fired and fired his high-powered rifle at the small figures in the car and done his duty as well as the others. But it was with disgust that the pair had created the necessity and at length he found it so disturbing, especially the day and night of waiting and the banshee death screams of Bonnie Parker, that it made his face look even more like the death's head it already had resembled.

Tex had not presented a threat to the public like Bonnie and Clyde, but the Rangers had discussed making an all-out search for him when he disappeared following the Blackland shootout. But they had had greater priorities and they circulated a notice that he should be picked up if his whereabouts became known. He was a high-grade criminal but a low-grade fugitive who until then had never killed anybody that they knew of but other shady characters. Some lawmen may be prone to a level of friendliness with well-known criminals who play the game intelligently and with a little humor and some had that kind of relationship with Tex.

Alerted by the report of chloroform, Tomes had two top investigators leave Austin and Texton for Terkel while he directed the hunt for Tex and other suspects. Ronni Dale's name came up with twenty other Wilkie associates. The Rangers fanned out to check them all and by nightfall found her apartment. She was at work and Tex did not answer the door. They found the bar she worked at and Ned was called in Austin when she told them yes, Tex was staying with her. They took her back, but he had left.

Tex was glad he was in Houston because he wanted to go to a nightclub he knew, Big Daddy's. He left ten minutes after the Rangers and took a cab. He was comfortable with Gene "Big Daddy" Cromartie, having let his hair down there two or three times. He had rarely been a heavy drinker but had considerable experience with drugs and once or twice a year would drug himself into oblivion by injecting heroin or a powerful pharmaceutical like a post-operative sedative if no heroin was available. He didn't do it often enough to be an addict and took care not to let it become a regular habit because he would have then had less credibility as a killer.

He went in and waited for Big Daddy because the six foot-six, two hundred-ninety pound black man could procure the heroin and two or three attractive women. He still had seven hundred dollars of Dr. Arnott's money and flashed some to motivate the bartender to send for Big Daddy.

Cromartie had been a nightclub man for most of his life and killed a couple of men himself. Tex and he locked eyes across the table with a look of what could only be described as mutual dark knowledge. "Well, sir, what can I do for you this evening?" he asked, shaking Tex's hand.

"Aw, I want some action," said Tex. The juke box churned out rhythm and blues as men and women danced, drank and talked. "Girls, heroin, clean needle."

Big Daddy filled Wilkie's requests along with a case of beer, some trucker's pills and an untraceable nearby motel room, having been told he was on the run. Tex usually had either booze and women or drugs because the drugs were so powerful, but he wanted everything at once tonight. He took a big shot of heroin at nine and a smaller one at three in the morning. He took pills to get from getting sleepy and the hazy, liquid experience of the drug never nudged him toward sleep. The beer tasted good because he was dehydrating and needed fluids. The room was sultry but reasonably well-furnished and comfortable.

It must have been the beer that did it because that was what he had the most of after three-thirty. He didn't typically drink a lot because a number of times he had gotten drunk and come close to killing someone when he did not want such a reaction. He killed a half-dozen black people and Mexicans on mean drunks in the early '30's and evaded punishment each time either by covering it up or because it was easy for a white man to get away with killing minorities in those days. At a little after five, he got out his lock-blade knife and grabbed the nearest woman by the hair.

The others looked at his brutal expression as he held the knife to Regina's throat, pinking holes in her neck with the hot-sharp tip and making her bloody. They had thought he was a mean-looking old man but were used to rough people and had had no indication he would get violent. Screaming and hitting with their arms, they fought each other to get the bolted door open and were further panicked by Wilkie's crushing up behind them and stabbing their backs and hips as he held Regina in his left hand, grunting like a beast.

The first two women opened the door and escaped. Not deeply cut, Regina broke away with a desperate application of strength, leaving a ball of hair in Tex's fingers, and ran faster than she had known she could, falling on the far side of the driveway but bounding up to find Big Daddy.

Cromartie knew who Wilkie was but knew he only had a knife and looked at it about the same as he would have with any old crazy dude. "Mister Tex?" he called through the open door. He had a .44 Derringer and he had been a boxer and might let him lunge, sidestep and clip him with a little knockout punch. "Can I come in?"

He nosed into the room and saw Tex standing on the other side where the beer was, drinking with the knife nearby on the floor. "I didn't hurt anybody, did I?" Tex asked.

"Naw!" Big Daddy asserted, smiling. "They all right."

Chapter Fifteen
"Whatta Ya Heard 'Bout 'Ol Hoodle?"

Ronald "Jelly" Barnes was one of the best lawyers in Texas. Six foot one and fairly trim with dark curly hair and a Boston Blackie mustache, he thought so hard and yet so fluidly that people could watch him think, moving his face and body and using his skills in a constant flow. He was a flawless courtroom tactician and an imaginative and moving speaker with a dominating presence. But as such attributes may, Jelly's drew as much opprobrium as praise. He was hated by lawmen, the families of his clients' victims and various other law enforcement-minded people because he was so often successful, in their minds, at thwarting justice. He took it with studied bemusement and a little grief, knowing, even if no one but his wife and other attorneys seemed to, what he was. He was obliged to make ethical allowances at times, but he was a lawyer, not a criminal, and it was regrettable that so many people didn't appreciate the difference.

Barnes was the first to learn whom Tex had given the money to. Tex never mentioned the man except when Jelly needed money and Tex would have the lawyer contact him. Tex had left fourteen thousand dollars in cash with a man he had known in the Huntsville prison, now a wheat farmer in southwestern Oklahoma, Hoodle Jones.

The Rangers got Ronni Dale to admit she had not seen Tex until mid-day after the crime. They traced him to Blackland, the garage and the borrowed car. The alley tread matched the tires, but it was a common type and the casts weren't good enough for court. So they could not prove he had been in Terkel. A particularly offended Terkelite offered to testify he had seen Tex in a cafe there that night, but the Rangers did not believe him.

They were further flummoxed by Ronni Dale, who disappeared with determination and some evident imagination, taking a few belongings and vanishing from Houston and, as far as the Rangers ever knew, from the earth. They made unsuccessful searches for her before each of the three trials.

They knew Wilkie had done it; they just couldn't prove it. He never testified, but his statement to investigators was often repeated in the newspapers: "Boys, I have an alibi, but I can't say who I was with that night because she's a married woman." The juries of hard-faced farmers in Terkel, Favorite and Whittle Nock over the next three years knew he was guilty, too, twice giving him the death penalty and the last time life. But each time, the state appeals court in Austin looked at the evidence and kicked it back.

The tormented Tomes drove himself through nights and weekends and even in his dreams. He whipped and lacerated himself to drive and drive, concentrate and push, think of nothing else until by virtue of his suffering new evidence would emerge, Tex Wilkie would be convicted and executed and the world would again be in order. He sat down after supper one night, got halfway up, made a half-cry to his wife in the kitchen and died, pitching over sideways with a final moan over the case.

They made Tex do hard time all right, keeping him in the air-tight new county jail in Blackland and basically on a bread and water diet for four years. Jelly protested, but the jailers always stayed just within the rules. Tex responded toughly and didn't complain. The sheriff and jailers harbored the hope he would break and admit Dr. Arnott had hired him, but he was a pro and that would have abrogated his whole history and whatever future he had left. He was still Tex Wilkie and that would have made him nothing. Because of what he had done and because they knew his convictions wouldn't stand up, they never let up on him. They saw it as loyalty to the Rangers and Ned Tomes, so they had him under one hundred-thirty pounds and looking snakier than ever when the third appeal finally came down and Jelly got him out on bail.

Tex was down to a level not even he had known he could reach. The days, months and years had been a fog of interminable discomfort and hunger, aching bones in the seemingly always cold cell, no cellmate and no one visible for hours on end, nothing to read, no cigarettes, no time outside in the fresh air, a chicken wire bed with no blanket, no mattress, no pillow and a bucket to defecate in that went unemptied for days.

It was a different Tex than had ever existed whom Jelly faced on the morning he got him released on ten thousand dollars' bail. The authorities were saying they'd try him a fourth time, but the delay would be longer and the bond denial was no longer tenable. "Whatta ya heard 'bout ol' Hoodle?" Tex asked, moving from side to side but keeping his eyes on the lawyer.

Jelly shrugged, gauging his client's response, and said, "I heard he bought three new combines."

Tex said nothing, did not react at all except that astonishingly, as pale as he was, he turned even paler.

Chapter Sixteen
"Hoodle and Tex"

Tex was on the loose and out of control like he had never been. They gave him back his lock-blade knife and he was going to gut Hoodle like a steer in his own living room. The news that Hoodle had betrayed him made something pop in his mind so that now, though maintaining an outward calm, he was on the attack in as blindly destructive a fashion as a bullet hawk or a fighting bull. He was so focused on reaching and killing Hoodle that he took no precautions at all.

Nobody ever knew if someone tipped Hoodle or if he was just edgy and watching. Whatever the reason, chubby little Hoodle Jones was ready when Tex flung open the screen door that morning and came in moving fast and stiff-legged like a monster. Hoodle was scared of Tex but was a tough guy himself, an ex-shotgun man in the bootlegger wars, and he knew that anybody, Tex included, would die if they walked in with him aiming his double-barrel sawed-off twelve-gauge shotgun. Squatted behind the cocked hammers and big barrels when Tex came in, he was like a boxer dispassionately delivering a one-two. He put one charge in Tex's chest and the other in his face. The buckshot reversed Tex's direction and blew him back into the screendoor. He fell onto his left side on the back of the doorway over the concrete porch.

Hoodle was overjoyed in his white frame house ten miles west of Big Toe Lake and twenty-two miles north of White Buck, Oklahoma. He could imagine his ghoulish fate had Tex gotten the drop on him. Wilkie's reputation was such that Jones only had to say he saw him coming and didn't know why Tex wanted to kill him to be exonerated. Throughout the tri-state region among lawmen and criminals who had crossed Tex and woke up in a cold sweat, the news was absorbed with exquisite relief and even pleasure, including at the dinner Jelly Barnes took his wife Georgia to that night.

Nine months after killing Tex, Hoodle opened his dynamite-rigged mailbox and died even faster. Whoever it was used a method that explained what it was about because Tex had pioneered in Texas the practice of dynamite-rigging cars.

The Arnotts kept to themselves and resurfaced only once more. The charge against Sarah was reduced to "aiding in the commission of a felony," for which she paid a fine and received a suspended sentence. The appeals court waited two years to reverse Harry's conviction because Judge Errol Nix had erred by allowing a distant cousin of Dr. Gill's onto the jury. He was retried another year later, anticlimactically after Tex's death.

Smiling often and laughing with his lawyers, Harry coasted through the trial, having only to contend with the Gills' affidavits, and got two years. He had taken care to bely the accusations in every way he could in Bosque and after nine months in which he helped to run the prison hospital and spent his free time painting landscapes, he returned to Bosque and Sarah.

A LONG WAY FROM THE LIGHTS

"A man feared that he might find an assassin;
Another that he might find a victim.
One was more wise than the other"--STEPHEN CRANE.

1

When Billy Ray Dooley daydreamed, it was about the great rodeo clowns, not the comedians and barrelmen with trained animals and exploding cars but the big bullfighters like Leon Coffee and Wilbur Plaugher. He wanted to be like them and was working with a small time clown, Maxie Goins, who managed a south central New Mexico ranch. Green eyes ablaze above his bulbous nose, painted orange on his purple face with red and yellow stripes, Maxie went at it spitting and cussing as the darkhaired Billy Ray, six foot two and two hundred-fifteen pounds, backed him up.

Each clown must have his own "face" or unique makeup and will challenge another whose patterns too closely match. Not yet having perfected his, Billy Ray used a light green base with blackened eye sockets and nose and blue and white stripes on his cheeks. He had an electric blue newsboy cap and fat man's overalls dyed orange and blue. Maxie sported an Oakland A's cap, an oversized Green Bay Packers jersey with Ray Nitschke's No. 66 and huge bright green shorts. They wore running shoes and made no comedic overtures apart from the costumes. A one time high school wrestling star, Maxie at least once a night ran and tried to hop a running bull's back, indifferent to taking a tumble, and often succeeded--impressive for a five foot eight man jumping off soft dirt.

They lived on Maxie's grandmother's ranch, the Double Bar G--twenty five thousand acres north of Los Vaqueros with a creek, water wells, two thousand head of Santa Gertrudis and Limousin cattle and a dozen oil wells. It was worth millions and to Maxie's worsening discomfiture, his uncle was questioning his honesty. Sure, he cooked the books a little and sometimes took calves to an auction two counties away because Grandma Dorothy was still in the 1960's, twenty years behind the times, in her view of what he should make. He could not get any oil money and needed extra for rodeoing, barhopping and paying on his two-tone blue Continental. Uncle Johnny kept coming from Texton in the lower Texas Panhandle, where he owned a prosperous tire store, to complain to his mother and brace Maxie. With a limp and a horn scar on his left cheek, Johnny had been a clown, too, and told Maxie he'd never be as good. "I know whatch're doin'," he said in the front yard Sunday afternoon. "Ya better pick up ya clownin' 'cause I mean to th'ow ya ass off this ranch! Momma won't disinherit ya 'cause o' ya daddy, but we cain't tol'rate ya rustlin'!"

Rustlers are the bane of the cattle business and being called one made Maxie livid. "Get outta here, you ol' bastard!" he shouted. "I'll beat the hell outta you!"

"Ya better bring ya big buddy if you try!" called Johnny,

getting into his black Cadillac with wire wheels. Rolling the window down as he backed out, he called in reference to his brother, Maxie's dad, "I'm sure glad George ain't alive to see this!" Firing rocks with seeming Major League velocity, Maxie cracked Johnny's windshield and nailed him in the trunk and back window. Johnny considered going back to fight but realized he would be humiliated. "You got a better way," he said to himself.

Maxie's grandmother was sentimental about family and would not have rejected him for purloining a few unregistered cattle. She was inside listening to a TV evangelist and did not hear or see the argument. But Maxie felt at a telling disadvantage against an older man whose mother had all the power.

Technically just a day laborer, Billy Ray had little going for himself. Having graduated from high school in Los Vaqueros five years after Maxie, all he had known how to do was play football, fight, drink and chase women. He was working at a car wash in Alamogordo when he saw Maxie at a rodeo and confided he would like to try clowning. He was thrilled the week after the confrontation with Johnny when they were doing a rodeo in nearby Philby for seventy five dollars a night each and Maxie moved over between bulls and asked, "Would you be interested in a lifetime job?"

Billy Ray threw himself between the next bull's horns, locking his hands around its neck in the melange of sweat, dust and manure scents. The crowd hooted as the brindle beast jerked his head up and down, trying to shed Billy Ray. It stirred Maxie's memory of a rodeo in Albuquerque when he was riding saddle broncs as a teenager. A skinny lefthanded cowboy in a white shirt, coming off the right side, got his gloved hand caught and the clowns could not extricate him. Brahma bulls crossed with Charolais, Herefords and Mexican fighting bulls do not normally go far from the chutes; but this one, incited by the cries of the rider and crowd, went all over the place, bucking more and more madly and even falling down and rolling over the cowboy, who was not freed until his arm tore loose from the shoulder. Maxie knew then and now that he would have done whatever it took to free the man, who died. Billy Ray let go and was tossed way up. He landed on his face and chest, bounded up with his arms raised and hollered at the top of his deep voice, "Wah hoo!" And he saw what stardom could be like when the crowd of fewer than a thousand people on Philby's western outskirts gave him a standing ovation, laughing, cheering and applauding for so long that the next ride was delayed.

2

"You love the Double Bar G, don't you?" Maxie asked the next day as they rode together.

"Sure I do," said Billy Ray.

"He cain't run it right from Texas, can he? I worked out here my whole damn life! Are you willin' to solve the problem?"

"Well, considerin' what's at stake, I'll do it."

"With a guaranteed job, you can concentrate on rodeoin.' I think you can make it big like the Kajun Kidd."

Maxie got a twenty gauge double barrel sawed off shotgun and told Billy Ray Johnny opened the store at seven a.m. Monday through Saturday, an hour before the employees came. He gave Billy Ray cash to rent a car in Roswell and told him the future of the ranch depended on him. "You gotta be tough," he said. "You cain't show weakness."

"I won't."

Billy Ray drove out late that overcast April Sunday night in his old brown Chevrolet pickup, rattling over the cattle guard at the road and heading east under a dim half moon. He had thought of taking marijuana but decided not to so he would not be arrested if he were stopped. He'd never expected to be doing something like this, but he was so in Maxie's thrall that he felt he would have nowhere to go if he failed.

He parked ten blocks from Avis in Roswell and slept until daylight, then walked to a cafe to kill time and went for the car at eight. Figuring the gold and white 1979 Ford LTD wouldn't be remembered in Texton, he used his driver's license. Maxie waited at the ranch with some trepidation but more cold anger while Billy Ray made his way under the speed limit across New Mexico and into West Texas. He passed Goins' Tire & Wrecker Service in Texton in the late afternoon, checked into a motel a mile away and carried in the suitcase with the gun and five heavy birdshot shells. He ate in the motel restaurant and stayed in the room all night, watching old western movies and a track meet. He knew Maxie thought he was dumb, but he was more thoughtful than Maxie knew, having applied his experience with football and rodeo to the assassination. Anytime he had something difficult to do, Billy Ray confronted his emotions in advance and settled them so when it came time to perform, he could do it with sangfroid.

He timed his arrival at six fifty-five. When Johnny unlocked the door, Billy Ray put the gun under his blue and silver Mustangs football jacket with No. 77 and three letter bars on the bottom of the "L" and walked over and in, triggering chimes that played, "The Eyes of Texas Are Upon You." He knew Johnny would recognize him, so he pulled the gun and shot him in the face from about a foot with Johnny resting his palms on the counter. It blew him backward onto the concrete floor, and Billy Ray put the gun under his coat and hurried out. Sobbing and retching, he summoned all his concentration to get out of town and over the Texton County line without hitting anything. A new employee found Johnny within twenty minutes and when police and some friends got there, one who knew him well exclaimed, "It was that damn nephew!"

Accompanied two days later by agents of the New Mexico Bureau of Investigation, the Texas cops went through the ranch entrance with the big iron Double Bar G brand overhead, found Billy Ray and took him to car lots in Alamogordo and Roswell until the Avis guy recognized him and gave them the rental and mileage records. Maxie was gone. Billy Ray had ridden his horse at three a.m. to bury the shotgun in a pasture and was unable to find it for the cops because he had re-leveled the soil and replaced the grass; but they traced the car to the motel, got the clerk to identify him and even found a guy who, while walking his Dalmatian, had seen Billy Ray leaving the scene.

The NMBI caught Maxie on a friend's ranch near Santa Fe. He hired a lawyer and fought extradition, but Billy Ray copped a plea and the Texas Attorney General's Office won the writ. Threatened with execution, Billy Ray accepted sixty years in the Texas Department of Criminal Justice. Maxie turned down seventy five and got ninety nine. Johnny's widow watched Billy Ray testify and gasped when he related the conversation in which he had agreed to do it. The defendants looked like what they had always been, Maxie furtive and mean and Billy Ray big and forlorn, shadowy now and a long way from the lights.

THE BLACKTHORNE TIGER

They came out the backyard gate two or three late afternoons a week, just before dusk, the woman in long shorts and sneakers, wearing a black and silver Blackthorne Panthers T-shirt and leading the Bengal tiger on a leather leash. The seven-month-old tiger weighed three hundred pounds and was over six feet long with its tail, and his master and he made a surreal sight in the park across the street, moving between the trees. The woman made a show of being at ease, waving at neighbors in their yards and speaking to adults and children if they were close enough. The tiger looked young enough to be still somewhat babyish, although some onlookers thought it could pull out of its collar, break its leash or drag the woman to attack someone, if not her.

A few were brave enough to approach and start a conversation, and she told them tigers raised from cubs, as this one had been, would not become dangerous. She said she had always loved animals and got to studying exotic pets. Her husband had a good job as a field supervisor for Hutton Oil Company and usually let her have her way; so they and their children, a fourteen-year-old boy and ten-year-old girl, paid fifteen hundred dollars for the newborn male and drove the two hundred-fifty miles to Dallas to get him. They bottle-fed him until he was ready for solid food and now his primary diet was raw chickens from the supermarket.

"He ain't ever offered to bite or claw any of us," she'd say. "My kids play with him all the time in the livin' room and backyard. You don't think I'd let 'em unless it's okay, do you?"

The story flew around the West Texas oilfield town of eleven thousand people. Some gave her the benefit of the doubt, but most thought she was kidding herself. Some had heard of or seen big cats like cougars kept in cages and sometimes briefly released. But no one knew of such an animal's having been kept in such a blase fashion. Someone called the Fitzhugh County Banner to say a family was raising a Bengal tiger as a pet and wouldn't that make an interesting article? People respected the couple, Jack and Alice Anglin, and liked their children, Ricky and Angie. But they thought Alice had gotten way off the beam and feared a terrible outcome.

Alice knew people were afraid of her tiger and was distressed when Ricky came home to say a boy at school had accused his family of "just wanting to scare everybody." So Alice eagerly accepted when Betty Flournoy, the Banner's lifestyle editor, called and asked to come over, see the tiger and do a story. With large color photos of the animal looking, some readers thought, rather crazed, the Sunday story landed like a bomb, showing the Anglin kids playing with it in the living room like the family dog let in for a romp.

Mayor Roger Beagley and other city council members had already been getting calls about the tiger but now absorbed a civic paroxysm, hearing that "the damn thing" was sure to kill somebody. Of course, the sight of a Bengal tiger advancing is one of the most terrifying in nature, implanted in Americans' minds from decades of movies with the black stripes working in yellow and white fur and the pupils widening in the orange eyes. The council had its regular semi-monthly meeting two nights later and went into a closed executive session to review its options with City Attorney John Eaglemeister, who was also Fitzhugh County's district attorney.

The tall, sharp-featured lawyer, a thunderous prosecutor who regularly got draconian sentences, told the councilmen they could pass an exotic animals ordinance, the consideration of the which was approved and a public hearing set. If passed, as though there were a doubt, it would prohibit, along with big cats, coyotes, wolves, badgers, bobcats, raccoons, skunks, monkeys, chimpanzees and other creatures normally considered wild. Fines of increasing severity could be imposed.

The hearing came in two weeks and the Anglins were prominent in a capacity crowd. Alice testified early, repeating her familiar arguments. "Tuffy is big," she said. "He can get over six hundred pounds and be ten feet long with his tail. But there are other big animals that nobody is afraid of, like a cow."

Ricky testified that he liked the tiger and was not afraid of it. He recounted the boy's accusation and emotionally stated that his family did not want to frighten anyone. A dozen citizens came forward to speak into the microphone with a few backing the Anglins but with most seeking the ordinance's earliest possible enactment. "I'm glad we don't live next door," a man said. "I might have to lean over the fence and shoot it!"

Mayor Beagley called on Eaglemeister. "Mayor, members of the council, esteemed members of the community," the attorney began. "Heaven knows we don't want to do anything in Blackthorne to interfere with any of the constitutional, statutory or inherent freedoms of our citizens. Texas always has been and I trust always will be a place where we have untrammeled independence. But we must consider the true nature of this circumstance. Ladies and gentlemen, I have studied it in depth and have discovered numerous cases in which wild beasts, thought to be tame, have, out of the wild blue and without provocation, turned on their keepers or bystanders and done their worst. We don't have to pass this ordinance. But we must consider in the most serious manner the fact that a Bengal tiger has the instinct and the capacity to destroy a man, and when it's done, it's done!"

He ended with a crescendo, growling the second "it's done" and shaking his jowls as though watching the Anglins' tiger eat the garbageman. That seemed the undisputed high point until a woman came to the podium and said, "Our son is about their boy's age and he kept disappearing after school with a couple of his friends. I went looking for them and looked over the fence and there they were in those people's backyard playing with that tiger. It liked to have scared me to death! They'd been daring each other to climb the fence and get in there with it when those people were gone. We put a stop to it, but if our kids did it, others could, too."

Alice came back to say she had had no idea that neighborhood children were playing with the tiger and that she didn't want them to. She promised to take steps to prevent it. Her husband sat in a corner and said nothing. The council approved the ordinance on first reading that night and on second reading two weeks later.

Everyone thought the Anglins would give up the tiger; but they sold their home, moved into the countryside and put it into a section of pasture enclosed in a ten-foot-tall steel fence behind their house. It could be heard growling at times and the neighbors worried it would get big enough to jump the fence. Jack and Alice had combed the enclosure to ascertain that it held no snakes, but one night the tiger found a diamondback rattler and, never having seen one, moved close to sniff it and was nailed on the nose. Alice proclaimed that the snake had been thrown over the fence by someone who hated the tiger, whose head was swollen big by morning. None of the veterinarians would come to treat it, and three days later, it died.

THE WAR

Drizzle thickened into rain, shushed through the leaves and grass and drowned the sough of the wind and chitter of the birds. One flew over a fence rimmed with barbed wire to the smokestack of a building and sat with his beak buried in his feathers. Guards walked the corridors between buildings or hurried tip-toe in the downpour.

Men inside a barracks near the camp's perimeter awoke to the squawk of a radio at the lighted end of the room. Static-interrupted silences and ebullitions of loud voices took their torpor from them. Orange dots appeared next to faces and cigarette smoke permeated the air. They dressed and moved past the bunks and through the door. The sun gleamed on their coats and on the broad plates of water on the ground. Scents of burnt bacon and bread filled the room where they ate at long rows of painted wooden tables.

Smears of earth melded like umber wax three thousand feet below. All that moved was the shadow of the helicopter fluttering over the uneven surface. The pilot moved his hand in a stirring motion on the curved control stick while the co-pilot slouched and watched the jungle; but the crew chief, sitting behind the pilot, was tense. "Again I want to see and do the things we've done and seen, where the breeze is sweet as Shalimar and there's forty shades of green," the pilot sang into his headset.

"Seen anything yet?" the crew chief asked.

"It'll show," the co-pilot said. "We still got a long way to go. Look for some white."

The pilot watched the quivering hands of the instruments and the landscape moving under them. The chopper varied little its flat, bumping flight. It was past mid-morning when the crew chief saw the wreckage: first a spot of white and then the jet aslant in thick trees. Branches whipped and dodged in the gush of wind as the chopper came down close with a rumbling clatter and whoosh. The men peered at the two dark forms one behind the other in the jet.

"We can't do nothin' for 'em," the pilot said. "The base'll have to send someone to get 'em out. We can't land and we don't have the fuel to wait around." He pulled the stick to his belly and the machine ascended gyroscopelike.

Insects' buzzing replaced the sound of the helicopter where the white plane lay. The insects crawled on and flew against the riveted sides and in and out through the broken glass of the cockpit, dotting the white helmets.

The men felt nothing when a bullet spun from the trees and pierced the chopper's metal skin and the bottom of its fuel tank. The co-pilot contemplated the circular steel roof of rotor blades and the pilot hummed in the key of the bass yowl of the engine. "Relax," the pilot said, turning half to the crew chief. "We'll be home in an hour."

The crew chief saw it first. The red fuel wand was dropping too fast and bouncing off the peg. "We're running out of fuel!"

"No, it can't," the pilot said. "We had enough." He looked from the gauge to the verdure ahead and moved his hand over the instruments as if to end the emergency like that. He brought the craft lower. The others tightened their harnesses and watched the pilot and gauge. He relaxed. "The gauge's messed up," he said. "That's the only answer." He shrugged, sharpened the rotors' pitch and fed fuel to the engine. As the helicopter neared its former height, the engine missed once, then twice more and died.

The crew chief strained against the straps and shrieked, "This is it! I'm! I'm!" The pilot caught his breath as the chopper lost its hold on the air; he tried to look over the floor without moving his feet. Then they were screaming and cursing as it dropped like a great, ungainly bomb, whistling powerlessly. He gaped at the rushing ground and tried to swoop with the machine and half a second too soon brought it up for its one landing. It leveled out a hundred feet above a partial clearing and fell hard, its landing pipes giving with the impact into a giant smile and gouging up chunks of grass and moist earth as it brokenly bounced to rest on its nose. The pilot coughed from the dust that puffed in. The co-pilot moved his head from side to side and moaned. Blood dropped from his mouth and chin. The crew chief hung forward in his harness; the pilot reached back and moved the youth's chin slightly with his thumb and index finger. He released his straps and the co-pilot's and they clambered out through the small side door on the left.

The co-pilot staggered and fell down. "Can you make it?" the pilot asked. The man shook his head. "Lassiter is dead and we've got to get out of here!" He looked inside the co-pilot's mouth and saw the tongue was deeply bitten a half-inch from the tip. "You can't just lay there," the pilot said, resting on spread knees. "They're coming!" He gave the co-pilot his hands and they stumbled-ran across the clearing. He ran back and tried the radio, but getting no response, he jumped out and returned to the co-pilot. He looked back at the helicopter several times before the jungle obscured his view.

A slow breeze came, striking the back of the machine and flowing around the bullet hole. The circle of spilled fuel shrank. The chopper groaned and swayed. It moved downward slightly and then fell with a rush of air, squatting heavily to its belly in the tall grass. Again it was motionless except for the slow bouncing of rotor blades. The radio twinkled with lights and prattled incoherently and a flamboyant bird at the jungle's edge squawked back.

Bullets burst from the trees and rode the air in minute descents to the bulk of the helicopter. Holes opened in the body and cockpit door and glass spiderwebbed in the cockpit cover. Four men ran with rifles across the clearing on the side opposite from the fugitives' trail. The chopper shook when they climbed into it. One stripped the dead youth of his watch and rings, pistol and knife, boots and the contents of his pockets. He gave cigarettes to the others, who loosened the radio and two heavy machine guns from their mount in the open sliding door.

The co-pilot lay off the trail under thick foliage a quarter-mile away, having been there since he had given up and the pilot carefully hid him. They tried to pick a place where it would be unnatural to walk and the pilot brushed out their tracks as he backed away. When the co-pilot heard the shots, he stiffened with dismay at the swiftness of the pursuit. He listened hard but heard nothing more except the cries of startled birds. He lay the side of his face against the leaf-sheathed ground and put his palms down flat beside his head.

The soldiers stripped the chopper quickly and walked into the jungle carrying their booty. The tracks were easy to follow till they came to a break in the overgrowth. They walked past the hiding place of the co-pilot, who stopped breathing and watched their legs. They went ten yards by and stopped where the tracks disappeared into a thick overlay of leaves. One went ahead to look. The co-pilot lay still and listened to the urgent conversation. The one who had gone ahead returned and directed his statement to a soldier wearing a blue cap. He pointed in the direction he had come from.

Three of the men were gone and the fourth made his way around the break in an ever-widening oblong. He moved slowly, keeping his rifle ready. He only took a step or two at a time and often stood still. The co-pilot reached for the pistol and extracted it moving only his arm. Despising his trembling, he pushed off the safety with his thumb. He depressed the trigger, pulled the hammer back as far as it would go and let the trigger out. He held the pistol off the ground in front of his face. After a long time, he began to feel steps upon the ground. He waited until the last moment before he would be seen and, extending his arm in a striking motion when the soldier reached to move a branch, fired the heavy pistol into the upper center of the youth's abdomen. The ground shook and the soldier, mouth gaping, flew backwards. Birds keened. The co-pilot arose and looked at the body and then the ground where the end of his tongue lay in red leaves. Ahead, the soldiers turned half toward the sound of the shot. The younger said something to the one in the blue cap and grinned. They moved on as fast as their burdens would let them. The co-pilot turned his attention and stooped slightly when he saw the enemy was dead. He looked all about his surroundings and for a long moment at the clouded sky. He bolted in the direction opposite from the one the pilot had fled in. Stiff-backed and hobbling, pistol in hand, he disappeared into the trees.

The pilot was jogging rhythmically when he heard the shots. He stopped and heard more. He stood and stood in the shadows of a tree whose branches sagged to the ground and finally turned, pushed off his right leg and began to run. Within a few strides, he was going as fast as the jungle permitted. He bent and turned for obstacles without altering his rhythm, breathing deeply and bringing his knees high. Things went by as if thrown at him. He tripped once in a sudden depression and fell on his arms and thighs in a flat bed of water. But he was instantly up, spitting water and slipping on the wet soles of his boots. He wouldn't concede fatigue, but within a mile he was heaving to the depths of his lungs. His knees would not come high. He ran blindly as much as he could, turning his thoughts to smiling women, galloping horses and green, rolling hills. The sole concession he gave to the running was to its rhythm. He ran another mile and another, moving little faster than a walk. The pain under his ribs bent him down. All his clothing was stiff with sweat and his feet slipped slightly from the moisture in his boots. He ran till his legs would barely part. He came to another hard-to-see low spot, fell and couldn't arise.

The soldiers hurried along the trail and saw it had been chosen without cunning. In less than an hour, they found where the boots had made long marks in the turf and where the pilot had fallen. They saw he had stopped running and begun to walk. It was early afternoon and they stopped to eat rice. Their quarry began to keep his fatigue more static by speed walking and jogging and briefly lying down when he felt too heavy. Insects swarmed him. Drawn by his sweat, they worked under his clothes and attacked his skin.

The pilot and soldiers remained equidistant through the afternoon. The soldiers neither ran nor rested. They ignored the insects and walked as though going down a narrow corridor. The sun went down on their right and they went on until dusk and made camp. After eating, they hid the things they had taken, hung hammock-like beds low to the ground from trees and covered themselves with mosquito nets.

The pilot followed his hands through the viscous darkness, moving his arms as if swimming. He fell by tripping over logs and vines and stepping into low places. He walked into thick brush and found another avenue without changing direction. His forehead hit a stiff, sharp branch and his face ran warm. He rubbed the pain and looked blindly at his hand in the dark. Animal sounds accompanied him, but he could not see the animals and after a while did not look for them. The jungle brightened when the moon took its place in the lower eastern sky. He mumbled and cursed and his arms swung out of time. He saw a layer of leaves under a tree and fell on it with a grunt, pulled his legs up and shifted his arms and head. The rocks softened and the ground breathed. His limbs were warm and heavy and he lay as stolidly as a root.

It was dark when he awoke, so he couldn't tell which way he had been going. He felt the ground for footprints and a clue. Rather than risk going the wrong way, he waited until sunup to start. A short way from where he had slept was a thicket of fruit trees and he took some fruit and ate it. He came to a stream and drank deeply. Now he walked rapidly and straight. Each stride felt good and he enjoyed his renewed strength. "They expect me to give up today," he said. "But they can't catch me if I don't give up and I won't. They're walking and I'm walking, so how can they catch me if I don't give up? I know they're not running."

The enemy would lose time, he knew, if they had to stop and look for his trail; so he sought hard ground, rocks and logs to walk on. At one point, he leaped to a low-hanging branch and swung hand over hand to another tree. He climbed into it and swung east on another limb over a pond where he dropped and walked a hundred yards on the sides of his boots. The heat was building again at mid-morning. The soldiers went single file ten feet apart. They came upon the pilot's bed and the man in the blue cap kicked the compressed dirt and leaves.

Sweat covered the pilot's body and insects stuck to his shining face. He heard people talking, saw peasants traveling and hid till they were gone. When the light waned, he realized his pursuers might speed up and he started running sporadically. For the first time that day, his breathing got labored. Like a runner at the finish, he went faster and faster. The earth blurred and tilted.

The soldiers quickened their pace because they had fanned out periodically to relocate the trail. The delays and the disadvantage of three men's chasing one had kept them from gaining ground. The one in the blue cap continued with a flashlight. They went on for hours after twilight softened the trees' edges and the night obliterated them. They would stop while the leader took the bobbing light in a circle to find the tracks.

One was an older man with wounds in his legs that had healed into deep scars. Cartilage popped in his knees and he sometimes fell or stumbled. They lost the trail again at a big tree and the leader turned off the light. He could not see the tree clearly but perceived its greater darkness. They ate and drank in silence. This terrain was flatter, so each man found a separate place. The old one did not spread his hammock but pulled the mosquito net over himself and relaxed into slumber.

On a partially exposed limb twelve feet above the ground and near the first thatch of leaves was a black flight boot. Close by was its mate. Two pillars of flesh widened from the boot tops to a torso and its appendages. The darkness was flawless and the pilot had only been able to see the soldiers' light. He had breathed very slowly as they made their beds and heard them breathing now. A pointed knur on the tree trunk gouged his back. His bent knees quivered. The night became cooler and impossibly blacker. The blackness had no bounds. He crossed his eyes and could not see his nose. Yellow-white and tumescent, the moon oozed up from the earth. It shone softly on the tree, the jungle's center, and made soft shadows. He ran his hand along his leg for the pistol, but the holster was empty. The two green marks across the circle of green dots said eleven o'clock. He touched the knife and took it out. The handle was hard and corded and the edge so sharp it felt hot.

The watch said one o'clock and two o'clock. It said three o'clock. The air was cool. An easy rain started to fall and a slow breeze chilled him. His legs were numb and his feet tingled. He silently arose and touched the tree. It was rough and warm like the limb on which he stood.

The leaves became more visible. The limb, wide near the trunk, began to assume its form. The rain stopped and the tree dripped. The pilot saw he was too much in the open and would have to move out into heavier leaves. Carefully, he took his left foot off the limb, reached his right leg out, and holding with his right hand in the fork of his legs, moved out. When he was a few feet from the trunk, the limb cracked. He shifted his weight and reached for support. It cracked again and bent enough to make him slide downward. He gripped the limb with all his strength and tried to keep from making noise. As it bent more, he remembered the knife; but he grabbed it too late to stab the tree, falling free with his hands out, and the blade cut through the old one's lung and split the heart.

The pilot lay hugging the dead man for a long time, then raised his head to look at the others. Their mouths were open! They were as slack as the dead one. Mechanically, he tip-toed and lifted his knees high. When he was even with the younger soldier, he smiled. He reached down delicately and tickled the soldier's nose. The youth slapped at the non-existent insect and the pilot smiled again, almost laughing, and gestured obscenely at the other soldier. Then he turned to the jungle, committing himself to it, and took two steps into a deep hole hidden in the leaves. He ran, wailing to the tops of the trees, but the soldier in the blue cap sat up and fired. The youth incredulously watched the one in the blue cap put down the rifle, walk to where the body lay, lean over and tickle the pilot's nose.

Some of these forty-nine poems have been in Poetry Life and Times, Decanto, Autumn Leaves, Machinery Press, Red Lion Sq., Ancient Heart, Poems Niederngasse, Refraction, Falling Star, Prism Quarterly, TPQ Online, The Smoking Poet, Ascent Aspirations and Jellyfish Whispers.

CARNATIONS

Raindrops
Plunge
To their deaths,

Splashing
Dust
Carnations.

MORNING

Slow air
Sweetly
Moist,

Darkness
Lightly
Peeling,

Wings of
Things are
Bustling,

Fecund
Soil
Fumes, and

Shadows
Shrink to
Hardness.

FROTH IS MADE OF BOULDERS

Sticks and froth shoot forward in the river.
Boulders sway and tumble on the bottom.
Even the fish cannot resist; they stop
Within the calms to let their colors bleed.

Even the bed and bank are soft to the river's
Rub and cut. Nothing the river touches
Holds itself in place. Sticks are bright
From river fish. Froth is made of boulders.

BLUE OCTOBER LIGHT

In every exhalation,
Every breath of blue,
The azure conjuration
Of the wind
Is changing hue.

The bluest of the patches,
Parlors of the sky,
Show bluer by the snatches
Of the clouds
Proceeding by.

The blue in the eyes of notions
In a face of pinkish white
Is as blue as the deepest oceans--
Blue
October light.

THE WOODS CAN YIELD THE STRANGEST BIRDS

The woods can yield the strangest birds
With cries and colors heretofore undreamed.
Flowing like a prophet's words,
The furious, cacophonous stream

Expresses an imperative unseen.
Is it with another world imbued?
The mingling blends of golds, greens,
Reds, browns, yellows, whites,

Oranges and blues splashing
Through the streaks of fading light
Flash out like tarpons thrashing in the sun
Or waves of time retreating to the night.

LIKE FIZZ FROM A DR PEPPER

Desire of blood, spectacle of ideal--
The flood lifts the flame to snowy peaks.
Mountain goats with sharp little feet
And prickly pink tongues come down to drink.
Hail pocks the river and they ascend.

The season is beatific and cannot be
Repeated. Streets of anger pull jaws
Masticating the cud of territory.
Whipsawed notions spray out like fizz
From a Dr Pepper on a hot, hot day.

CONTEMPLATING SUICIDE

"Contemplating suicide" is an insufficiently
Considered expression because you
Don't contemplate suicide; it contemplates
You. The guilt, the guilt, how potent
It becomes, how subtle the overdose.

The knife, with the surgical steel blade
Made in Japan, where they've always known
How to make blades--you imagine the knife's
Cutting through the veins, muscles,
Arteries, how awful it is, yes, yes!

CRESCENDOING THE SHOW

Through the autumn haze
And a glow of greenish lights,
I hear the sounds of guitar music,
Noticing it's right.

They've left a window in the living room up,
The bass is thrumming low,
And the singer sings of an old lost love,
Crescendoing the show.

On a nighttime walk through the neighborhood,
Listening as I go,
The singer sings of an old lost love,
Crescendoing the show.

EMILY

Come away from that second-story window,
Emily. Lay your white dress across
The chair. I have read your poetry
And love you. Let us make this afternoon
A new world lasting long as we may live,
And you will know I love you for the beauty
Of your soul and the way it fills my heart.

NOTHING, NOW
(After Stephen Crane)

A rich man who had been born poor
Died and stood at the River Styx
In the Land of the Lost.
Squinting across, he asked Charon,
"How much will this cost?"
With oar groaning across the prow,
The boatman answered, "Nothing, now."

THE FLOATING SPECK

1
Our craft is ready now.
The waters take the ledge.
All on which we stand
Must melt away and all
Our longing evanesce
Like mist in the morning sun.

We must give our breath to fire,
Our thirst to brine, and sit
Like stacked stones while the blind
And blinding eye revolves
And rises through the dawn
At a place we guess in darkness.

We shall see unanchored islands
Pitching, plunging, each
Unknown to the other. One
Will have grass and sloping sands
And palm trees on the lean,
Another lichen scrolls

On the flats of granite walls.
We shall not ever stop
At them because regardless
Of our meaning, we would only
Bump against the rocks
Or be stranded upon the shore.

Our time will carry by
Like wind without a sail.
We shall have no minutes or weeks
Or years to celebrate,
Only days to float askew
Or bob up and down in a spin

And no escape but the side
Of the boat and the shoreless sea.
And we shall have days to believe
We are on the edge of a scream
Unending, infinite days,
When the sea is suddenly still. . .

2
Steaming orange and red,
The sun sets ahead.
And so the sun
Will show it's done,
And we shall walk
Among the waves--
Perhaps enfold
Ourselves
In a stopped crest

And rest.

A star descends, a star descends,
Not plunging forever through the abyss
Nor exploding rocket-like to end,
It is worn away by what surrounds it
Into just a floating speck
Of what there was, into nothing.

I LOVE THE POET GERARD MANLEY HOPKINS

I love the poet Gerard Manley Hopkins.
Constrained by his high calling, he wrote on napkins
As the other priests ate in the church
Chow hall. The words and rhythms would lurch
And leap like a whale harpooned and protesting fate
While he was known for picking at the clerical plate
And smiling benignly to his brethren before
Composing another tumultuous line. The lore
Of ancients lined his life, but the Wreck of the Deutschland
Was a modern event; and Hopkins with a steady hand:

"A love glides lower than death." Of course
The magazine editor for the church was a horse,
And he told the diffident poet the poem did
Not meet current requirements. Duty said
To put aside indulgences and pray
Without ceasing, and so he did until he lay
On a stone bed and died at forty-four,

Poetic voice stilled and soul sore
From imperfection, conflicting God and art,
Conflicting the immortal spirit and the human heart.

ELIJAH-JOHN
THE BAPTIST

Elijah, when he ran from Jezebel,
Having lost composure after he had slain
Four hundred-fifty advocates of Baal,

Dejected by his flight across the plain,
Asked God to take him from this evil world,
For Ahab's queen had proved herself the bane

Of the holy prophets sent there by the Lord.
Elijah had been zealous, but his fear
Prompted this ironic exchange of words:

God asked, "Elijah, what're you doing here?"
Then said, "Now go outside while I pass by."
A mighty wind, an earthquake and a fire--

But then a whisper as the Lord came nigh
Put 'Lijah on the path that Enoch walked:
The only two men who didn't have to die.

Ahab and Queen Jezebel had stalked

The men Jehovah sent with His commands,
But because the Tishbite never balked,

The end of her would come by eunuchs' hands:
Face-first to the cobblestones and hooves
To be dolloped out across the land

By a pack of dogs. Watching from the roofs,
The peasantry took in the hellish scene
As the great adulteress proved that it behooves

Everyone to understand God means
What He says. Don't subtract or add a thing
To Scripture, not even to please a king or queen,

For we have seen what happens to the kings
By example after example in the text.
It was time for the chariot to bring

Elijah home to Heaven and for the next
Prophet of the Lord to take his place.
Elisha now would doubly move to vex

The enemies of Jehovah and His love.
Elijah would return as John the Baptist,
Awaiting Him who merited the dove

While living on wild honey and some locusts.
Baptizer of the Savior of Mankind,
He came back yet again, transfigured with Moses.

Elijah-John the Baptist, yes, would find
And testify of the Savior of Mankind.

GIDEON'S FLEECE

Searching for his bravery,
Gideon was a skeptic, telling
An angel and the Lord his clan
Was the least in Manasseh and he
The weakest of his brethren. He asked for a sign,
And the angel waited until he could design
An offering. Gideon's plea
Was answered with fire, and he took his stand
As leader of the nation, felling
Midian and slavery

And giving Israel forty years
Of peace. With, of course, the guidance
Of the Lord, three hundred who
Had lapped their water like dogs
Chased an army of one hundred-thirty-five thousand,
Took Zalmunna-Zebah captive and
Punished Peniel and Succoth. The logs
Of Peniel's tower toppled and O
How Succoth suffered for the stridence
Of her unpatriotic jeers!

Before they blew their trumpets, broke
Jars and shouted, "A sword for God
And Gideon!" the leader asked
For signs night after night to moisten
Fleece and leave the ground dry, then wet
The soil around dry fleece to show the bet
Was on. Forty-three pounds of choicest
Gold were given to the task
In Ophrah of making Gideon's ephod.
Worshipped, it became a yoke

To the patriarch and all his people.
Gideon died at a good old age
And as soon as they had lost their sage,
Baal-Berith was on their steeple.

THE GHOST, MELCHIZEDEK

Into the vale of the human wreck
Drifts the ghost, Melchizedek.
In his native garb, he sniffs
Mephitical smoke along the cliffs,
Hears the demons babbling madly,
Turns his face and shields it sadly
As the demons and the king,
Juxtaposed, fulfill the ring:

This far into our lives, less
Enthralled are we to contemplate the coming
Purity than to hear and feel the humming
As it heightens with such a subtleness
That we perceive the changes in a kind
Of retrospect. And it is not a pit
Nor something we fell into. The gist of it
Is in converging circles in the mind.

Do we deserve, O king and priest, the blessing of your hand?
What now do we owe for what we are?
Abraham is not among the flowers of the land,
And you have heard the muses, the bizarre

Voices that we hear.
If you would touch me,
I could veer
Sublimely, swiftly
Far from here!

THE GATES OF JERUSALEM

1

Artaxerxes Nehemiah served.
Cupbearer to the king, he was concerned
That the walls of Jerusalem were broken down
And all the city's portals had been burned.

With Artaxerxes' blessing and his letter
Telling the forest keeper to yield the wood,
Nehemiah rode from Susa ready
To start the work the Spirit said he should.

The Valley Gate, the Serpent Well, the Refuse
Gate and walls, the Fountain gate, Jeshanah
Gate, the King's Pool and the towers fell to
The brethren's hands. Sanballat and Tobiah

Despised the cause, laughed at "the feeble Jews"
And tried to stop the work; but Judah came
Together as one man, saying, "We will
Restore it as you say." The Arab Geshem

Joined the Horonites and Ammonites
And accused Nehemiah of suborning
A rebellion. But the leader refused to run
And finished on the fifty-second morning.

Whaling their way toward the House of Heroes,
The goldsmiths Uzziel and Malchijah
With Zadok the son of Baana and Jehrico's men
Joined the perfumer Hananiah

At the Broad Wall, East Gate, Water Gate, Horse Gate, Fish
Gate, Sheep Gate, Inspection Gate and the Wall of Ophel,
Fixing the parts at the Ascent to the Armory
And resurrecting the Towel of Hananel.

The Law was read by Ezra the priest in the square
By the Water Gate. A feast was held and then
A meeting where the Levites prayed, recounting blessings
And asking God's forgiveness for the sins

Of the people--their stiff necks and stopped-up ears.
"You gave them kingdoms and nations," they said, "but they
Grew fat and disobeyed, cast down your Law,
Killed your prophets and sinned against Your Way.

We'll make a sure covenant and sign it. Our leaders and priests
Will seal it." So they did. But Nehemiah
Returned, rebuked Eliashib and ejected
From the courts of the House of the Lord Tobiah.

Humbly asking God to be remembered

For good, the builder made his history.
Preaching the Word after the Crucifixion,
Peter and John explained the mystery

Of salvation for everyone. They went to the Gate
Called Beautiful at the Temple at three p.m.
And said, "All those who repent and are baptized
In the name of Jesus Christ will live through Him."

A crippled beggar asked for alms, but Peter
Commanded, "In the Name of Jesus Christ, arise!"
On his feet and praising God, the man
Leaped through the Beautiful Gate. Caiaphas' spies

Tried to turn the crowd and called the priest;
But the forty-year-old man held onto them
Who had summoned the power of God to end his woes
And skipped through the loveliest gate in Jerusalem.

2
Solomon's Colonnade was where
They took this pivotal affair
In the story of Christianity,
Peter and John, the apostlery,

To tell the throng the Son of God,
Rejected, flogged and crucified,
Afforded all the promise of
Salvation and Jehovah's love.

Elders, teachers of the law
And rulers called them forth and saw
They were uneducated men
Who'd walked with Him who had no sin.

Filled with the Spirit, Peter said
The One arisen from the dead,
The holy, righteous Lamb of God,
Now holds Heaven's staff and rod.

"If we be struck by the chastening hand
For a good deed done to a helpless man,
Know it was through the sacrifice
And power of the Name of Jesus Christ

That he was healed," he said. Let go,
They returned to the colonnade and lo,
Five thousand in their absence had
Believed and the church was being added

To each day--the bride of Him
Who had come to the gate in Jerusalem.

THE SEVEN SONS OF SCEVA

Sons of the priestly Sceva, they
Were exorcising people when
An evil spirit in a man
Answered as it heard them say,

"By Paul and Jesus, we command
You, come out and go back to Hell!"
"Them I know but all too well,
But who are you with such demands?"

The demon asked. Then the one
In whom it dwelled rose up and thrashed
The seven sons, beat and bashed
Them bloody and naked until they ran

Out of the house. The story spread
In Ephesus and fear went through
Magicians among the Greeks and Jews,
Who piled the sorcery books they'd read

And burned them in the sight of all,
Fifty thousand silver, confessing

The Name of Jesus Christ and blessing
The work of His Apostle Paul.

FAITH SUSTAINS THE AMISH

Faith sustains the Amish on
The highways of Pennsylvania.
At eighty miles an hour, the traffic
Passes the buggies by.

Anonymous whip, slow motion horse,
Black buggy fabric state that
Slower is not just better, it's
The only way to fly.

Of course, occasionally someone's drunk
Or the road's too slick and death comes,
And you think of how philosophy
May sometimes lead to this.

In most respects, they're right about
The evils of the modern;
But how can they trust that the cars and trucks
Are always going to miss?

THE GIRLS OF SHILOH

Reclaiming his unfaithful concubine,
A Levite from the hills of Ephraim
Spent five days with her father, making merry,
Before departing in fear of Jerusalem.

They put into Gibeah, where a man,
Alarmed, said, "You can't stay in the city square."
As soon as they had washed themselves and eaten,
A crowd of the depraved besieged them there.

"Give us the man who came of late!" they shouted.
The old man begged his townsmen, "No!" and offered
To make his daughter go, but the mob roared on.
The Levite and his host finally proffered

The concubine, who suffered all night to
The death. Her master cut her up and sent
A piece to each of the dozen tribes. Asking,
"Who has heard of such a thing?" they went

To the Benjamites to demand the guilty but were
Refused. In that time of judges, there was

No king, and so from Dan to Gilead
And Beersheba, four hundred thousand for the cause
Took up arms, inquiring of the Lord, "Who shall
Go first?" He sent Judah, and on Gibeah's
Sand the truculent tribe of Benjamin slew
Twenty-two thousand. The Spirit's advice to lay

An ambush at Baal Tamar finally
Reversed the fight, and fifty thousand fell.
The last six hundred Benjies fled and made
Their stand on the Rock of Rimmon. The Scriptures tell

A tale of national insanity,
For the victors voice their grief all night and ask
God why a whole tribe should be missing, then
Because Jabesh Gilead is absent, task

Twelve thousand to slay those brethren, too, and bring
Four hundred virgins for the rebels, who,
Still two hundred shy, are told to lie
East of the road to Shechem for the Shiloh

Girls, absolving their fathers of the oath
That none would ever join the scandalous tribe.
When the girls come dancing out, each man
Grabs one and takes her home, and as the scribes

Impart, peace is restored. The cataclysm
Over, there is little else to say of it
Except to repeat it was a time of judges,
When every man would do as he saw fit.

THE MOST BEAUTIFUL WORD

"Cuspidor," James Joyce averred,
Is English's most beautiful word.
Eschewing the romantic, "Mary,"
"Crystalline," "pristine" and "aerie,"
"Amaranthine," "alpenglow,"
"Whippoorwill" and "mistletoe,"
The maestro used his ear and wit
And said it's a can where people spit.

WHERE HE ISN'T GOING

Dante Alighieri went to
Hell in dreams each night
And wrote of it in terza rima
For us to share the sight.
Popes and princes, of course the rich,
By dint of what they do
Are all consigned and the enemies of
The poet live there, too.

Hell is but the first leg on
His journey to Paradise,
And what a surprise to learn the lowest
Circle is caked in ice!
Souls in ever-worsening situ-
Ations the lower you go
From the Virtuous Pagans to guys like Judas
Who betray the people they know.

Getting through such a place requires
A guide and not just any --
For Dante the poet Vergil, who
Is ancient in 1320.

The Harpies are bad, the Giants are worse,
Medusa makes them quake,
And they never lay eyes on Hecate,
The Lady of the Lake.

They climb their way back to the top
Up Satan's hairy chest,
And Dante bids farewell to Vergil
To let him take his rest.
The night is clear, the stars are out
And time remains for knowing
The essential truths, the main one being
Where he isn't going.

THE WOOLLY MAMMOTHS

Beloved of God, they trod the floes
And poked their tusks through icy ages.
Shaggy, slow, their mounds of muscle
Made the meals for mankind's stages.

Jingling down their icy sides,
The woolly mammoths shambled through
Their unrecorded history
And white world, one or two

At a time trapped by hunters creeping
Up. The matings, doubtlessly,
Were the happiest interludes--
The fragrant lover beautifully

Voicing her affection after
The tusky chasing of a rival.
The time came for the ice to melt
And put at risk the beasts' survival.

The pachyderm was a favorite of

The Father's, so he led a remnant
To the haven of Russia's Wrangel Island.
Animals never circumvent

His will. That's what makes them holy,
In a sense. No longer behemoth,
Down to five feet high at the shoulder,
They nonetheless retained their mammoth

Ways from when the world was colder:
The truculence of the bulls, the fuzzy
Ladies' ambience, the calves'
Tentative strength, learning the many

Uses of a trunk. Half-size
And less from the times of foggy snorts
And hungry hunters, the compact little
Things continued shrinking, not

Dying out so much as fully making
The most of the circumstances, steered
By their Creator to the place
Where at length they disappeared.

THE EMPEROR IS A POET

I will not bow but only shake
Your hand, as is my way,
Because I come from the wide, wide land
That's called America.

We fought your troops on the islands of
The Pacific in World War II,
Learning what the Bushido
Of the Rising Sun could do.

There was a civil war in the 1600's
In Old Japan
With some of the factions of the Shoguns
Wiped out to the man.

Firearms copied from Chinese's
Caused most of the slaughter
As showdowns flowered 'mong Samurai
Who had trained to give no quarter.

So the Shoguns called a halt to this
And gathered up the guns,

Telling the Japanese that it
Was a trend whose course was run.

Then the days of peace and beauty
Returned for several centuries
Till Samurai in the military
Condemned all things Chinesish.

Now you live in the Land of Lotus
Blossoms, as you know it,
Where politeness is the way
And the Emperor is a poet.

HONK TO MAKE
THE BUZZARDS FLY!

Honk to make the buzzards fly
As you traverse the Great Southwest.
Gourmets of guts, they're loathe to leave
The fecal stench of their repasts.

No, not eagles and not cranes,
Bedraggled wingspans black as sin,
They launch reluctantly, the weight
Of moist satiety on them.

Maggot- and intestine-glutted,
Packed like Dumpsters, buzzards need
Consideration of their hygienic
Value and exigencies.

Heavy, yes, and slow of wing,
They fly too late unless you warn,
Sometimes to the windshield only
Sans the sounding of your horn.

Bursting buzzard, bursting glass --
If you know worse, then spare the lie.
You're fifty miles from town, remember:
Honk to make the buzzards fly!

WHAT ONLY DUCKS CAN UNDERSTAND

Big duck's walkin' on the big lake shore
And doesn't mind givin' other ducks what-for.
Well, it's "quack-quack!" and "quack-quack!" that.
There is no doubt who wears the big duck's hat.
He swims out in the water and then drifts in to the land
And tells the other ducks what only ducks can understand.

THE POLITICIAN'S WEAKNESS

The politician's weakness
When he goes to play the fiddle
Is the predilection for playing
Both ends against the middle.

THE ROBIN WHO IS BOLDER

The pods of April manifest
Themselves upon the branches
And out across the ranches,
The mares begin to foal. The best

Are up and running within minutes.
You can tell which ones have got
The speed -- knock-kneed at first
But then a burst of speed. In its

Ancestral need, it keeps up with
The mother, traveling farther
In a day than the young of other
Species. The only reason life

Is dull is the fault of the beholder.
We don't perceive the brightness;
We cannot hear the rightness
Of the Robin who is bolder.

THE FIRES ON DOLORES' MOUNTAIN

The mountain where Dolores mourned her lover
By setting a fire each week
For thirty years is a monument to duty.
She trudged up to the peak
South of Fort Davis, Texas, each Thursday night
With firewood or a hatchet
To stoke the blaze and show
How much she mourned Jose.
Folks who claimed to know

Said she was driven mad by the shock of learning
That he, tending sheep
The night before their wedding, was scalped and murdered
By Mescaleros. To keep
Her promise and do something praiseworthy
For him, she made her way
To the breezy top and lit
The first fire. People
Soon came to know that it

Was she who wore a trail from the settlement west
To the mountainside,
And in the 1860's a broken heart
Or even a broken mind
Was a good enough excuse. Misunderstood,
I feel, she gathered wood
And matches and became
A legend no one bothered,
For there could be no blame

Attached to this. Today the mountain seems
to stand for them, the star-
crossed couple, and when you drive or hike Dolores'
Trail, you see how far
She had to go those solitary nights,
Aiming for the light
To show there was no counting
Stars or the love that burned
In the fires on Dolores' Mountain.

THE POETIC IMPULSE

Every time I think of how much room for memory
There is in the loose girdle of soft rain,
I think about the one who flew through
The Brooklyn gates and wrote on them, "Hart Crane."

I have read, I think, most of his poetry, and all of it is good,
If not overall at least in certain parts:
Poetry of a type that was not done again from the time he wrote
Until the exclamations of Delmore Schwartz.

Both of them died alone and without a notice, come to think
Of it, alone in abject circumstances,
Crane over the side of a boat and Schwartz from booze
For who knows what perception of squandered chances?

The biographers tell us problems of a personal nature led him to take
That leap off the Continental Shelf;
But any artist knows the pull of the void and knows the poetic
Impulse is disturbance in itself.

THE BEAUTIFUL WHITE SPATS

How can Slick Slack heal his heel,
Bruised by a worn-out loafer,
Chilled in the gurgling gutter,
Aggravated by the pull

Of a tender tendon? He limps a lot
Each morning, but new shoes
Ameliorate the abuse
Of sidewalks during the day. Not

For lack of circumspection does
Slick's heel stay sore.
The mornings of before,
When his physicality was

Flowing from his feet--nostalgic,
Rueful memories
Of well-being, geez,
A contrast to Slick Slack's neuralgic

Truism of the stride that
Is poignant in the extreme.
Boy, the memories seem
Beautiful like the white spats

Of a Jazz Age gent striding forth
Onto Forty-Second
As the lady beckoned,
Luminous in their mutual mirth.

POOR BOY'S BLUES

The rich get richer and the poor get screwed--
Barefoot scrapper with face contused,
Ol' bronc rider with his backbone fused,
Broke ol' lady gets her name confused
An' says "howdy doody!" to the dog abused
By the boy next door that we've excused
For the beatin's he takes to keep daddy amused.

The rich get richer and the poor get used,
Kids go hungry while the old men brood,
Girls get crazy and the boys tattooed
(Gotta change the meanin', gotta change the mood);
Got no money when you can't buy food,
Got no honey 'cause I'm actin' rude--
Poor boy singin' for the blacked and blued.

THE TARANTULA'S BRAIN

Things, including me, are slow
Like tarantulas in Old Mexico:
Bad to see and worse to know,
Clod to post to alpenglow--

Colors cool, mirage that is
Soothing to the mental fizz
That clouds the tarantula's brain and his
Is nowhere near the current whiz

That I'm contending with. Free it
From your boot and let it be. It
Runs for its life, as might befit
A creature you kill when you first see it.

WHAT IT IS
THEY LEAVE WITHOUT

Upon the pure white screen,
Reflections of selections
Of something for everyone:

The people sit apart and yet together,
Adoring a woman who wears an ostrich feather,
Hum with the singer and move in their seats with the dancer
And cry for the blond-haired man who dies of cancer.

Diffusing, merging, babbling, flowing,
They slide and bump politely, going
Through the out-flung, sweating doors,
Through, outside to the streets and stores,

Departing in doubt
But blending so well
They cannot tell
What it is they leave without.

LOOK!

With you, I play in flowerbeds
And sleep in easy chairs.
Look at me and make me see
Myself perusing you,
Talk to me and let me feel
Your voices in my throat.
Laugh at me and make me feel
The same consuming mirth.
I find the depths of me to be
Revolving in the sun.
It's warmer than I remembered. Look!

THE CONQUERING
OF SPACE

I fill my life with open space.
Doing that is not so big a problem
As I used to think. The face

Of a crazy man shows it robbed him
Of his courage, but he probably
Never knew either to bob or swim,

Depending on your air. The gravelly
Demands of a father watching from the bank
Should spark an anger, however sloppily

Expressed, that brings you out of the tank
And puts you heaving, pulsing with egotism
For which you have ridicule to thank,

On the bank. Such things create a schism
Between fear and knowledge, between despair
And contempt for obstacles. "Yes'm,

I'll feed the little pigs right there
In their own trough and won't let any get killed
By the big 'n's, be sure and put 'em where

They won't get trompled, let 'em get filled
Up much as they want. You won't have to whup
My legs with stingin' nettle!" Tilled

With the right industriousness, kept up
Dutifully, the land is bountiful.
From the fattest steer to the scrawniest pup,

No form of life shall it annul,
And you will never want if only you
Will do your duty. A belly full

To stretching is your reward. As do
The headlights shaking over the road and jouncing
Their fragility in contrast to

The stillness of the stars, I'm bouncing
From the edge of the sky to the ground and finding a place
That only I can see. The trouncing

Of my resilience is a trace
Of my advancement. I put it down to movement
And the conquering of space.

RAIN RIMS
THE COFFEE CAN

Rain rims the coffee can on the porch outside,
And the night is rinsed pure black to the last crack
Of memory. Drooping faces look out from my eyes,
Passion remembered in the coldness of the dark.
Animals yelp from unexpected hurts, sounds
Disperse in the rushes and explosions of the drops.
Come in out of the rain, everything. I don't have
Anything to do but watch the water spilling.

THE KITES

The sand was hot along the ditch
And in the field, shaded in the leaves,
The clodded earth was cold.

The kites were shivering
As we arrayed them in the wind.
Tied with sticks and strings and rags,
They balked at first, climbed crookedly
As we ran across the rows,
And finally they flew,
Snake tails working them up, high,
Above the drooping lines.
"The wind is stronger high," we'd say,
Flipping our string-wrapped boards.

Hours were things we held
And let out as we liked.

When we tired, he stared for awhile
And said, "Lots of string to roll."

"Let's cut 'em loose," I said.

We wrapped our palms with the lines and cut,
Held on for a moment, pulling
The pull, looked and let them go.

RUNNING THE MILE

Not being warm on a chilly day
Is jarring me to the back of my head
For the first three hundred yards.

I do not feel the urgency
My arms and legs express.
"Sixty-three," my ally calls,
And I have to say I'm gliding.

I wish I could remember
How it was
I told myself to run.
The last is hard.
"Two-fifteen!"

The third is when I might let up,
But the others are holding, too.
My legs are emptying.

A sprinter's feet approach,
And a little one strains past
And goes in front.

"Three thirty-five!"
My critic yells.

I drive my knees and trail my heels
And stream exhaustion out my fingers.

The rolling fields are green,
The air is smoky hot;
Somebody is beside me--
Crunch around the turn.

How am I doing this? I ask.
Don't fall, I say.
So where's the line?
I'm out!

THE CONTESTANT

He jerks against the rope and bores
His weight into the back. The beast,
Twitching, kicking, slams the boards.
Summoned by his amplified name

And by the people's faces,
The contestant grunts and skids
Astride the gliding twists
To course the white lights
That are colored bright in shadows.

He grips the pain in his gloved right hand,
Slips aside by slow degrees--
Out of rhythm, mouth an O--
And falls down to the hooves and horns.

The crowd gasps in the air
Of the earth and in the space,
A red spot grows on white
As he looks in supplication
To the smiling face of the clown.

MY LEG BONE

My leg bone is solid stone,
My skull immortal steel.
My fists are made of marble
And destroy but do not feel.
My eyes are clouded, burning opals
Vaporizing tears.
My heart is a pulsing star, and I
Should live a thousand years.

But something in me knows
My guts are Cheerios,
My brain a rubber bowling ball
That cannot know the way
And my heart a doubled, kicking frog
On the verge of death today.

THERE WAS A STRANGE WRITER NAMED KAFKA

There was a strange writer named Kafka
Who didn't go in much for hotcha.
He stayed home alone and wrote with a moan
'Bout things that come till they gotcha.

HARRISON BLACKTHORNE

Harrison Blackthorne shaves his toes
And watches where his money goes.
The money goes into a store
That's known from Phoenix to Baltimore.

From Phoenix and Baltimore they come
For measurement by the Blackthorne thumb.
The Blackthorne thumb, the Blackthorne clothes
Make sure more money comes than goes.

More money comes than goes and he
Is written in the Registry.
Now written in, he is warm but wary
And none of the help ever calls him Harry.

None calls him Harry even though
He asks them all please to do so:
"Please do" to customer and friend
And always with a quarter to lend.

With quarters to lend for drink or phone,
He never has to be alone;
Yet daily alone as six o'clock chimes,
He locks every lock in the store three times.

THE SUPER CHIEF

Rocks beneath the rails
Creak as though they'd break
If the Super Chief should stop.

The wheels turn over one
Behind the other, clacking
The rails, heating up
And wearing themselves out.

The horn of the Super Chief
Blares ludicrously because
The rails are six inches high
And easily tripped over.

The train must follow
The rails, which could be heard
Groaning under the weight
If it were not so noisy.

THE NIGHT BIG AL AND THE BOYS WENT DOWN TO THE ADONIS SOCIAL CLUB

Al Capone was starting out
With Torio in Illinois
When he decided to hang out in New York for awhile
And have some fun with the boys.

Peg-Leg Lonergan was holding court
At the Adonis Social Club,
Saying "not enough guineas" had been given the pennies
Among the two score that he'd rubbed.

Irish girls and Italian boys
Met Lonergan's wrath as he said,
"Come back with a white man!" chasing them out,
His face turning redder than red.

With Needles Ferry and Aaron Harms
And several others, he stayed
Till word reached Big Al, who collected his pals
And of course to the Adonis soon strayed.

It didn't take long. They came in, sat down,
The lights went and all heck broke loose.
The gunfire, as it turned out, was all from Al's boys.
Lonergan's gang was cooked goose.

Peg-Leg was sprawled off the burlesque piano
With sheet music scattered around.
Needles and Aaron and two or three more
Were here and there dead to be found.

Capone said, of course, he didn't know what had happened;
He had just been around for some fun.
He was so little known, he was pegged for the doorman
When the newspaper stories were run.

It was just around Christmas and Big Al had fun,
And he went back to Chi-town contented.
"An Italian is whiter than an Irishman," he asserted.
"It was time that that buzzard got vented!"

THE LAST LONG RIDE OF JESSE JAMES

Harken, settlers! The rustic poet declaims
About the last long ride of Jesse James.
Wood Hite, a kinsman, o'er the cut from the Blue Cut Job,
Took on, alone, the Ford and Liddel mob;

Shot Liddel in the leg, but Bob Ford from behind
Pulled the same trick he pulled later on Jesse's mind.
He rode out from Missouri to Kentucky and back,
But the people at the boy's home were also in the black.

Dick Liddel was away somewhere, but the Ford boys were around
And Jesse planned with them to rob the bank in old Platte town.
Zerelda, Jesse's mother, warned him not to trust the Fords;
But he thought, she's an old woman, and ignored his mother's words.

You know the rest about the guns and the picture on the wall.
The public thought it a sickening thing to see Big Jesse fall.
Bob Ford was not a coward; he was a killer without a code.
He lost the draw to Ed O'Kelley at the Colorado Lode.

Jesse Junior was the clerkish type and Frank became a barker.
The Youngers rotted in Minnesota; Charley paid his marker.
But I wonder about the people who saw and met him on that ride,
A killing man who nonetheless was famous for his pride.
He took his last long ride to fight for Woodson Hite, his cuz,
And I will bet everyone he met knew who or what he was.

BILL QUANTRILL HAD AN OLD HORSE NAMED CHARLEY

Bill Quantrill had an old horse named Charley--
Actually not old but a runner.
When he cut the big tendon that they named for Achilles,
Quantrill said that his days had a number.

They caught him asleep in a hay loft, of all places,
And the horse of Miss Betsey was shying.
Shot down in the mud with his trigger finger gone,
He was paralyzed and soon would be dying.

The name was still his, but the body was gone.
He waited to die in Kentucky.
William Clarke Quantrill was a name that they knew.
He had always been heretofore lucky.

WHAT BONNIE PARKER MUST HAVE THOUGHT WHEN SHE SAW OLD METHVIN'S TRUCK

On the one hand it was inevitable,
On the other perhaps an illusion,
For after all, they still ran free
With the cops in apparent confusion.
Clyde Barrow had thought he might go on forever
As long as he had them out-gunned.
He had Bonnie Parker and a fast gray Ford coupe
And he knew he could keep them out-run.

They had been to the showers and ran spic and span
On the morning Frank Hamer lay waiting.
At sixty they came to the top of the hill,
Then saw what'd been left for their baiting.
Bonnie Parker was always more watchful than Clyde
And she worried as he slowed the car down.
He was doing what most country people would do,
But old Methvin was nowhere around.

Clyde still considered himself one of the folks
And Bonnie was a one-man woman.
She let him keep going till they stopped by the truck
And by then was too far in the omen.
She finally screamed; Clyde went for his gun--
The toughest bad character running.
Three pair of lawmen in the grass at the rise
With BAR's, too, started gunning.

They took it and took it, Clyde's BAR jammed
And he somehow came up with a pistol.
They did the death dance, the whole thing was a trance;
Enormities splattered like crystal.
It wasn't the end of the controversy;
The cops were the fugitives now.
Folks saw they had to take Clyde that way,
But they couldn't explain Bonnie somehow.

Young Methvin did time in McAlester's pen,
But he never was tried back in Texas.
With a restaurant in time for the second world war,
He was back in Louisiana for business.
But he never could shake it, that Bonnie and Clyde
Were dead so that he could be living.
He came to his end at the head of a train--
Avenue to a worldly forgiving.

Loud Raymond Hamilton went to the chair.
Only W.D. Jones made it through.
Nine of the dozen the gang killed were cops,
So you see how the coverage flew.

The dubious logic made out of it all was romantic,
Yes, that was the caper:
"A gritty ex-con" with a beautiful woman
And poems 'bout them in the paper.

With your life on the line, you fight to the end;
It's a thing that we all understand.
But seeing it carried as far as it was
Fascinated the average man.
The guns and the guts and the rural mud ruts
Are all now a part of history,
The summers they tried to catch Bonnie and Clyde,
When all of the blacktop was blistery.

There can be no way for a poem like this one
To find satisfactory conclusions
Except inasmuch as the game in the clutch
Has a way of embracing confusions.
Bonnie died second before standing up
In the arms of Ted Hinton--a gasp!
Clyde lay back happy 'twixt seat and the door,
Having once more evaded the grasp.

Children came quickly to dip in the blood
And look at their fingers of crimson.
A dozen farmhands had leaped from a truck
And made their way out of the jimson.
A long line of cars followed Bonnie and Clyde
In their hell-blasted car to Arcadia.
People came by the thousands through the funeral parlor--
A mob fit for several stadia.

Their families took them home to Dallas
And put them in separate ground.
The crowds again were catastrophic;
Revenge tales made the rounds.
Some of the story was well-known fodder,
Some of it only guessed;
And with it the ineffable,
Something that can't be expressed.

BURY MY HEART AT WOUNDED KNEE

Bury my heart at Wounded Knee
And leave me to eternity;
But never turn from the memory.
Bury my heart at Wounded Knee.

In South Dakota long ago,
Some people died that you should know.
Their cries were scattered in the snow
In South Dakota long ago.

They were people who were free.
They did not have to own to be;
And yet they owned all they could see.
They were people who were free.

In a circle there below
The guns and horses in a row,
They lay like leaves the wind could strew
In a circle there below.

Bury my heart at Wounded Knee
And leave me to eternity;
But never turn from the memory.
Bury my heart at Wounded Knee.

BILLY THE KID'S LAST DANCE

Billy the Kid was a wild Irish boy
From the rundown streets of Manhattan,
Coming by way of Arizona
New Mexicans' hatches to batten.
Some say his notoriety is not much deserved,
But I say 'tis well he's respected.
He liked the gunplay and the Mexican maidens
And there never was a pal he rejected.
Billy looked like a kid but was tough as hard leather;
He could ride a rough saddle forever.
Quick in his movements, lithe as a snake,
He could shoot you and laugh 'bout it after.

Pat Garrett was a smart one, figuring Pete Maxwell
Was the key to Billy's protection.
He knew, somehow, Billy would come to Pete's bedroom
Each night for a quick salutation.
Paulita, Pete's sister, was a problem and Billy
Was staying close now that he'd killed 'em,
Olinger and Bell, the ones Lincoln County'd
Had watching him till he could thrill 'em.

But the rope never held much attraction for characters
Like Garrett or the tigerish Billy.
He waited for the right time to move and he got 'em,
Then went out and talked Lincoln silly.

The foothills of New Mexico
Are a beautiful place for a man to die
With the deeper blue of the mountain sky
And fissures of the drifted snow.
Fight for land like this and find
The darker places in your heart
Where enmity and murder start
And passions of the moment bind.

Neither was tough; he got Bell with the handcuffs
And waited for Olinger loaded.
Importunately loud, Olinger caught it
When the two-barrel ten gauge exploded.
They were not the first; there were eight or ten more
And who knows how many uncounted?
To Billy 'twas horseplay, though seriously countenanced
And most satisfactory when mounted.
One interesting aspect of the war and the time after,
Though usually not much considered,
Is that Billy rode with and faced off with some people
As bad as or worse than he figured.

Rudabaugh, Roberts, Garrett and Bowdre--
They all got their shots in or better.
Kinney and Dolan, Frank Baker and Spurlock
Were in it, too, all to the letter.

Most of the people pitched in and took sides,
Largely on relatives' bases;
But many took Billy, seeing that he was
Bereft of a power oasis.
He had many friends, but they weren't the kind
Who could help with a trial or a ploy.
They rode with him, laughed with him; some even died
With him, failing to stay with the boy.

Companions of the dubious sort
Will lead an upright youth to ill,
But the livelier disposition will
Go further than from where they start.
Friends are friends who love your life
And shield you from the killing wind
And agents whom avengers send
To seek you with the gun and knife.

Lew Wallace was writing "Ben Hur" and he thought
That Billy was detritus best wasted.
"I gave him his chance," he opined, "but Bill Bonney's
A phenomenon unfortunately fated."
Garrett to his credit gave Billy a chance,
Waiting to draw till the throwdown.
With the Thunderer in one hand and a knife in the other,
Billy never did think he would go down.
"Who is it?" he whispered, not knowing 'twas Garrett
Till too late, he thought to shoot him.
A blast to the middle and he was well-wounded
Before the Colt pistol could scoot him.

The women were wailing and showed love for Billy
By standing up candles around him
On a bench in a work hut in the dark of Fort Sumner
With the righteous and wicked surrounding.
He had hid in the yard after traversing pasture
And waited till midnight brought safety,
Then run up in sock feet, armed and expecting
That once again, he would prove crafty.
The bedroom of Maxwell was one place in the world
Where Billy didn't want to do battle.
Garrett and Poe were hoping they'd get him
Before he had sense to skedaddle.

There is no place to run for those
Pursued by trackers of the kind
Who shrewdly choose and await the time
When they can overwhelm their foes.
In the shadows, they bide the night,
Letting the fugitive play on.
When the dancing ends and friends are gone,
They come at last into the light.

For Billy'd killed cops and the New World was waiting
To see how much longer he'd fade 'em.
He was so notorious that not in Old Mexico
Or even the East could he evade 'em.
Romantic and doomed, he went to the dance,
Or baile as folks then would call 'em,
Hoping the fiddler or man on guitar
Would somehow prefigure to stall 'em.
Leaping up here and swirling around there,

In boots and sombrero he charmed 'em
And no thoughts of jail breaks or shootouts or posses
Or anything else could alarm them.

The time was when Garrett would have been dancing with him,
Quick Billy and the tall, regal sheriff,
Not knowing that before two years passed they would meet up
And set off a cascade of grief.
He danced on and on, his boot heels commanding
The beat of the music to sway 'em.
They remembered in watching that Billy had never
Been one to let anything dismay him.
He was the most helpless, although the most dangerous;
For him nothing'd ever been right.
They put up the candles and guitar and fiddle,
And the dancers told Billy goodnight.
Yes, the dancers told Billy goodnight.